WORKBOOK

FOCUS ON GRAMMAR

A **HIGH-INTERMEDIATE** Course for Reference and Practice

SECOND EDITION

Marjorie Fuchs
Margaret Bonner

Longman

FOCUS ON GRAMMAR: A HIGH-INTERMEDIATE COURSE FOR REFERENCE AND PRACTICE
WORKBOOK

Pearson Education, 10 Bank Street, White Plains, NY 10606

Editorial director: Allen Ascher
Executive editor: Louisa Hellegers
Director of design and production: Rhea Banker
Development editor: Randee Falk
Production manager: Alana Zdinak
Managing editor: Linda Moser
Senior production editor: Virginia Bernard
Production editor: Christine Lauricella
Senior manufacturing manager: Patrice Fraccio
Manufacturing manager: David Dickey
Cover design: Rhea Banker
Text design adaptation: Rainbow Graphics
Text composition: Rainbow Graphics
Photo credits: **p.6** PictureQuest; **p.16** AP/Wide World Photos; **p.22** AP/Wide World Photos; **p.52** AP/Wide
   World Photos; **p.126** Kobal Collection, **p.146** AP/Wide World Photos

0–201–38306–3

1 2 3 4 5 6 7 8 9 10—BAH—04 03 02 01 00

CONTENTS

ABOUT THE AUTHORS

Marjorie Fuchs has taught ESL at New York City Technical College and LaGuardia Community College of the City University of New York and EFL at the Sprach Studio Lingua Nova in Munich, Germany. She holds a Master's Degree in Applied English Linguistics and a Certificate in TESOL from the University of Wisconsin–Madison. She has authored or co-authored many widely used ESL textbooks, notably *On Your Way: Building Basic Skills in English, Crossroads, Top Twenty ESL Word Games: Beginning Vocabulary Development, Around the World: Pictures for Practice, Families: Ten Card Games for Language Learners, Focus on Grammar: An Intermediate Course for Reference and Practice, Focus on Grammar: A High-Intermediate Course for Reference and Practice,* and the workbooks to the *Longman Dictionary of American English,* the *Longman Photo Dictionary, The Oxford Picture Dictionary,* and the *Vistas* series.

Margaret Bonner has taught ESL at Hunter College and the Borough of Manhattan Community College of the City University of New York, at Taiwan National University in Taipei, and at Virginia Commonwealth University in Richmond. She holds a Master's Degree in Library Science from Columbia University, and she has done work toward a Ph.D. in English Literature at the Graduate Center of the City University of New York. She has contributed to a number of ESL and EFL projects, including *Making Connections, On Your Way,* and the Curriculum Renewal Project in Oman, where she wrote textbooks, workbooks, and teachers manuals for the national school system. She authored *Step into Writing: A Basic Writing Text* and co-authored *Focus on Grammar: An Intermediate Course for Reference and Practice, Focus on Grammar: A High-Intermediate Course for Reference and Practice,* and *The Oxford Picture Dictionary Intermediate Workbook.*

UNIT

1

SIMPLE PRESENT TENSE AND PRESENT PROGRESSIVE

1 SPELLING: SIMPLE PRESENT TENSE AND PRESENT PROGRESSIVE

Write the correct forms of the verbs.

Base Form	Third-Person Singular	Present Participle
1. answer	answers	answering
2. ask	asks	asking
3. begin	begins	beginning
4. bite	bites	biting
5. buy	buys	buying
6. come	comes	coming
7. dig	digs	digging
8. _____	does	_____
9. _____	_____	employing
10. _____	_____	flying
11. forget	_____	_____
12. _____	has	_____
13. _____	_____	lying
14. manage	_____	_____
15. _____	_____	promising
16. _____	says	_____
17. study	_____	_____
18. _____	_____	traveling
19. use	_____	_____
20. _____	writes	_____

1

2 SIMPLE PRESENT TENSE AND PRESENT PROGRESSIVE

Complete these conversations with the correct form of the verbs in parentheses.

1. **AMBER:** I _____think_____ I've seen you before. _____ you _____
   a. (think)   b. (take)
   Professor Bertolucci's course this semester?

   NOËL: No, but my twin sister, Dominique, _____ Italian this year.
                                                          c. (study)

   AMBER: That _____ her! I _____ her name now. You two
                          d. (be)   e. (remember)
   _____ exactly alike.
        f. (look)

2. **JARED:** _____ you _____ that woman over there?
                                a. (know)

   TARO: That's Mangena. She _____ an English class at the Institute.
                                      b. (take)

   JARED: Mangena. That's an interesting name. What _____ it _____?
                                                              c. (mean)

   TARO: I _____. Let's ask her.
              d. (not know)

3. **ROSA:** How _____ you _____ your name?
                              a. (spell)

   ZHUŌ: Here, I'll write it down for you.

   ROSA: You _____ unusual handwriting. It _____ very artistic.
                  b. (have)   c. (look)

4. **IVY:** Hi. What _____ you _____? You _____ annoyed.
                          a. (do)   b. (seem)

   LEE: I _____ to read this letter from my friend Herb. His handwriting
              c. (try)
   _____ terrible, but he never _____ his letters.
        d. (be)   e. (type)

5. **AMY:** _____ you _____ to hear something interesting? Justin is a
                          a. (want)
   graphologist.

   CHRIS: A graphologist? What exactly _____ a graphologist _____?
                                                                                b. (do)

   AMY: A graphologist _____ people's handwriting. You can learn a lot
                              c. (analyze)
   about people from the way they _____, especially from how they
                                        d. (write)
   _____ their names.
        e. (sign)

6. **KYLE:** What _____ you _____ these days, Sara?
                                      a. (do)

   SARA: I _____ an article about graphology.
              b. (write)

   KYLE: Really? I _____ a book about graphology. I _____ it's a
                          c. (read)   d. (think)
   fascinating subject.

3 SIMPLE PRESENT TENSE AND PRESENT PROGRESSIVE

Complete this article with the simple present or present progressive form of the verbs in parentheses.

Right now Pam O'Neil ____is taking____ a test, but she _____ it.
　　　　　　　　　　　　1. (take)　　　　　　　　　　　　　　　　2. (not know)
She _____ about what she _____, not about how her
　　3. (think)　　　　　　　　　　　4. (write)
handwriting _____. The person who will look at the test is a
　　　　5. (look)
graphologist—someone who _____ handwriting. Graphologists
　　　　　　　　　　　　　6. (study)
_____ that a person's handwriting _____ something
7. (believe)　　　　　　　　　　　　　　　8. (tell)
about his or her personality and character. These days, many businesses

_____ graphologists to help them decide who to hire.
　9. (use)
What exactly _____ company graphologist Perry Vance _____
　　　　　　　　　　　　　　　　　　　　　　　　　　　　　10. (hope)
to learn from applicants' writing samples? "I always _____ for clues to
　　　　　　　　　　　　　　　　　　　　11. (look)
possible behavior," he explained. "For example, the slant of the writing usually

_____ a lot. _____ the writing _____ to the left or to
12. (tell)　　　　　　　　　　　　　　　13. (lean)
the right? A left slant often _____ a shy personality. The position of the
　　　　　　　　　　　14. (indicate)
sample on the page is also important," Vance continued. "The right-hand margin of

the page _____ the future. Here's a writing sample from an executive who
　　　15. (represent)
right now _____ a new direction for a large company. Notice that this
　　　16. (plan)
person _____ much room in the right-hand margin. This is the writing of
　　17. (not leave)
someone who never _____ looking at the future."
　　　　　　　　　18. (avoid)
　"What about signatures?" I asked. "Yes, signatures _____ us a lot about
　　　　　　　　　　　　　　　　　　　　　　　　　　19. (show)
someone," said Vance. "Look at this one by a chief executive officer of a large firm.

You _____ about him in the news these days because the government
　　20. (read)
_____ his company. Those very large strokes are typical of a person who
21. (investigate)
_____ about himself first and _____ advantage of other people.
　22. (think)　　　　　　　　　　　　　　23. (take)
　Vance always _____, however, that his analysis _____ an
　　　　　　　24. (warn)　　　　　　　　　　　　　　　　25. (not guarantee)
applicant's future job performance. There's no substitute for careful review of a

complete application.

❹ EDITING

Read this e-mail. Find and correct ten mistakes in the use of the simple present tense and the present progressive. The first mistake is already corrected.

---

                    aren't
Justin—I hope you ~~don't~~ feeling angry at me about my last e-mail. Remember that I

wrote, "I not want to hear from you again! '-)" That little symbol at the end means,

"I'm winking, and I only joke." We using a lot of these symbols in e-mail. We are

calling them emoticons because they show how we are feeling at the moment.

Here are some more:

:-)   I smile.

:-D   I'm laughing.

:-(I'm frowning.

8-]   Wow! I really surprised!

(:: ( ) ::)   This is meaning, "I want to help." It looks like a Band-Aid.

:-C   I'm not believing that!

Please write back soon and tell me that your not angry. ((((Justin)))) Those are hugs!

Delia

SIMPLE PAST TENSE AND PAST PROGRESSIVE

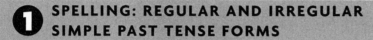

1 SPELLING: REGULAR AND IRREGULAR SIMPLE PAST TENSE FORMS

Write the correct forms of the verbs.

Base Form	Past Tense
1. _____agree_____	agreed
2. _____apply_____	applied
3. be	_____was_____ OR
	_____were_____
4. become	_____
5. develop	_____
6. _____	ate
7. _____	felt
8. get	_____
9. grow	_____
10. live	_____
11. _____	met
12. _____	paid
13. permit	_____
14. plan	_____
15. say	_____
16. _____	sent
17. sleep	_____
18. understand	_____

2 SIMPLE PAST TENSE, PAST PROGRESSIVE, AND *WAS/WERE GOING TO*

Complete the magazine article with the correct forms of the verbs in parentheses. Choose the simple past tense, the past progressive, or **was/were going to**.

First Meetings

by Rebecca Hubbard

*W*hat ___were___ you ___doing___
                       1. (do)
when you first _____ that special person
          2. (meet)
in your life? A few months ago, we _____
                     3. (ask)
couples to tell us about themselves. _____
                        4. (Be)
it love at first sight or _____ you

_____ each other? _____
5. (hate)
you _____ someone else before you
      6. (marry)
_____ your One True Love? Read some of the great stories from our readers.
7. (find)

*D*ana and I sure _____ in love at first sight! We _____ in the
          8. (not fall)   **9. (work)**
same office when we _____. At the time the company _____
          10. (meet)   **11. (hire)**
me, she _____ to get a promotion. It _____ my first job. I
     12. (try)   **13. (be)**
_____ scared, so I _____ to know everything. Of course,
14. (feel)   **15. (pretend)**
Dana _____ I _____ to get the promotion instead of her.
     16. (think)   **17. (want)**

One day I _____ on a problem when she _____ into my office. I
       18. (work)   **19. (come)**
_____ her for help, but I was stuck, so finally I did. And guess what? She
20. (not ask)
_____ it! So then we _____ competing with each other and
21. (solve)   **22. (stop)**
_____ in love instead.
23. (fall)

*V*an and I _____ the same high school social studies class when
              24. (take)
we _____. We _____ friends right away. At the time, I
    25. (meet)   **26. (become)**
_____ someone else, and Van _____ interested in a romantic
27. (date)   **28. (not seem)**
relationship. One day the teacher _____ me while I _____ to Van.
                                   29. (hear)   **30. (whisper)**
Because of that, we both _____ stay after school. I _____ about
                         31. (have to)   **32. (complain)**
such a severe punishment, but I _____ my mind because staying late with a
                                33. (change)
friend _____ so bad. That afternoon, we _____ talking. As soon
       34. (not be)   **35. (not stop)**
as I _____ with my old boyfriend, I _____ Van out.
     36. (break up)   **37. (ask)**

*A*leesha _____ into the apartment next door when I _____ her
          38. (move)   **39. (see)**
for the first time. I _____ on the front steps while she _____ a
                      40. (sit)   **41. (park)**
U-Haul in front of the apartment building. As soon as she _____ out of the
                                                          42. (jump)
truck, I _____, "I'm going to marry that woman." I _____ her out
         43. (think)   **44. (ask)**
right away, but a guy _____ her move. He _____ like her
                      45. (help)   **46. (look)**
boyfriend. But I _____ my plan to marry her. One day, I _____
                 47. (not give up)   **48. (run into)**
Aleesha and her "boyfriend" in the hall. She _____ me to her *brother!* I
                                             49. (introduce)
_____ her to dinner the next weekend.
50. (invite)

❸ EDITING

Read this entry from Aleesha's journal. Find and correct ten mistakes in the use of the simple past tense, the past progressive, and **was/were going to***. The first mistake is already corrected.*

December 16

                   decided

I'm really glad that I ~~was deciding~~ to rent this apartment. I ~~won't~~ wasn't going to

move here because the rent is a little high, but I'm happy I did. All the

            seemed

others ~~were seeming~~ so small, and the neighborhoods just ~~weren't~~ wasn't as

beautiful as this one. And moving wasn't as bad as I feared. I was

                           from

planning to take more days off work, but then Hakim offers to help.

                      moved

What a great brother! We ~~were moving~~ everything into the apartment in

                           seems

two days. The man next door ~~seemed~~ really nice. On the second day, he

even ~~help~~ Hakim with some of the heavy furniture. His name is Jared. I

did not

~~don't~~ even unpack the kitchen stuff last weekend because I was so tired.

         was walking

Last night I ~~walking~~ Mitzi for only two blocks. Jared was standing

                  was looking

downstairs and ~~looked~~ at his mail when I came back. I was going to

~~asked~~ him over for dinner this weekend (in order to thank him), but

everything is still in boxes. Maybe in a couple of weeks . . .

PRESENT PERFECT, PRESENT PERFECT PROGRESSIVE, AND SIMPLE PAST TENSE

1 SPELLING: SIMPLE PAST TENSE AND PRESENT PERFECT

Write the correct forms of the verbs.

Base Form	Past Tense	Past Participle
1. become	became	become
2. bring	brought	
3. choose	chosen	chosen
4. delay	delayed	
5. feel	felt	
6. find	found	
7. finish	finished	
8. get	got	
9. graduate	graduated	
✓ 10. hide	hid	
11. move	moved	
12. notice	noticed	
13. own	owned	
14. read	read	
15. reply	replied	
✓ 16. rip	ripped	
17. show	showed	
18. speak	spoke	
19. throw	thrown	
20. wonder	wondered	

② CONTRAST: PRESENT PERFECT, PRESENT PERFECT PROGRESSIVE, AND SIMPLE PAST TENSE

Look at the reporter's notes about the bride's and the groom's families.
Then write sentences about them, using the words in parentheses.
Choose the present perfect, present perfect progressive, or simple past
tense form of the verbs. Add any necessary words to the time expressions.

THE SKOAP–POHLIG WEDDING BACKGROUND INFORMATION

	Bride	Groom
○	Nakisha Skoap	Simon Pohlig
	born in Broadfield	moved to Broadfield in 1992
	lived here all her life	bought Sharney's Restaurant in 1994
	B.A., Claremont College, 1994	basketball coach for Boys and Girls Club
	1991–Began working for	1997–1999
	Broadfield Examiner	author, Simon Says and Duck Soup,
	1997–became crime news reporter	kids' cookbooks
○	and started Master's Degree	in Jan., started developing local
	program in Political Science	TV show
	started research on articles on crime	Mother–Tina Pohlig, president of
	in schools in Jan.	TLC Meals, Inc., for two
	Father–James Skoap, joined the	years, but plans to retire soon
	Broadfield Police Department	
	in 1979, retired in 1999	
○		

1. (Nakisha Skoap / live in Broadfield / all her life)

   Nakisha Skoap has lived in Broadfield all her life.

2. (she / graduate / from college / 1994)

   She graduated from college in 1994.

3. (report / crime news / 1997)

   Reported crime news in 1997.

4. (recently, / research / articles about crime in schools)

   Recentlty researching articles about crime in schools.

5. (work / on her Master's Degree / 1997)

   worked on her Master's Degree in 1997.

6. (her father / work / for the Broadfield Police Department / twenty years)

   Her father have worked for the Broadfield Police Department for twenty years.

7. (Simon Pohlig / move / to Broadfield / 1992)

   Simon Pohlig has moved to Broadfield in 1992

8. (own / Sharney's Restaurant / 1994)

   Owned Sharney's Retaurant, in 1994

9. (coach / basketball / for the Boys and Girls Club / two years)

   Have coached basketball for the Boys and Girls Club for two years.

10. (write / two cookbooks for children)

    Has Wrote two cookbook for children.

11. (plan / local television show / several months)

    Have planned local television show for several months.

12. (the groom's mother / serve as / president of TLC Meals, Inc., / two years)

    the groom's mother has served as president of TLC Meals, Inc. for two years

3 PRESENT PERFECT, PRESENT PERFECT PROGRESSIVE, AND SIMPLE PAST TENSE

Look at Nakisha's job application. Then complete the personnel officer's notes, using the correct form of the verbs in parentheses. Choose between the affirmative and negative form.

CODEX MAGAZINES JOB APPLICATION

1. Position applied for _____ Editor _____   Today's Date: <u>Nov. 12, 1999</u>

2. Full legal name <u>Skoap-Pohlig</u>   <u>Nakisha</u>   <u>Ann</u>
   Last   First   Middle

3. Current address _____ 22 East 10th Street _____

   <u>Broadfield,</u>   <u>Ohio</u>   <u>43216</u>   How long at this address? <u>5 months</u>
   City   State   Zip Code

4. Previous address _____ 17 Willow Terrace _____

   <u>Broadfield,</u>   <u>Ohio</u>   <u>43216</u>   How long at this address? <u>1968–June 1, 1999</u>
   City   State   Zip Code

5. Education. Circle the number of years of post high school education. 1 2 3 4 5 6 ⑦ 8

6.

Name of Institution	Degree	Major	Dates Attended
1. <u>Claremont College</u>	B.A.	Journalism	1990–1994
2. <u>Ohio State University</u>	——	Urban Studies	1996
3. <u>Ohio State University</u>		Political Science	1997–present

   If you expect to complete an educational program soon, indicate the date and type of program.

   <u>I expect to receive my M.S. in Political Science in January.</u>

7. Current job. May we contact your present supervisor? _____ yes <u>X</u> no

   Job Title <u>Reporter</u>   Employer <u>Broadfield Examiner</u>

   Type of Business <u>newspaper</u>   Address <u>1400 River Street, Broadfield, OH 43216</u>

   Dates (month/year) <u>9/91</u>   to (month/year) <u>present</u>

8. In your own handwriting, describe your duties and what you find most satisfying in this job.

   <u>I am currently a crime reporter for a daily newspaper. I write local crime news. I especially enjoy</u>

   <u>working with my supervisor.</u>

1. I __'ve interviewed__ Nakisha Skoap-Pohlig for the editorial position.
   (interview)
2. She __have applied__ for a job on November 12.
   (apply)
3. She __has worked__ at the *Broadfield Examiner* for a long time.
   (work)
4. She __have found__ that job while she __was__ a college student.
   (find)   (be)
5. She __has attended__ two schools of higher education.
   (attend)
6. She __began__ classes at Claremont College in 1990 and __received__ her
   (begin)   (receive)
   B.A. there.

7. Then she __went__ to Ohio State University.
   (go on)
8. She __have attended__ Ohio State University for three years.
   (attend)
9. At Ohio State, she __took__ Urban Studies.
   (take)
10. She __got__ a degree in Urban Studies, though.
    (get)
11. After a year, she __decided__ to study Political Science instead.
    (decide)
12. She __havent received__ her Master's Degree yet.
    (receive)
13. She __have lived__ at Willow Terrace most of her life.
    (live)
14. For the past five months, she __is living__ on East 10th Street.
    (live)
15. The company graphologist __looked__ at her application yesterday.
    (look)
16. He says that in question 8 of the application, Ms. Skoap-Pohlig __have leaved__ a space
    (leave)
    between some words when she __mentioned__ her supervisor.
    (mention)
17. She probably __hasn't told__ her supervisor yet about looking for a new job.
    (tell)
18. In her answer to question 8, she __slanted__ her writing to either the left or the
    (slant)
    right.

19. The graphologist __told__ me yesterday that this indicates clear and
    (tell)
    independent thinking.

20. The graphologist __suggested__ that we contact this applicant for another interview.
    (suggest)

4 EDITING

Read this letter to an advice column. Find and correct fourteen mistakes in the use of the present perfect, present perfect progressive, and simple past tense. The first mistake is already corrected.

Dear John,

 have been making
My son and his girlfriend ~~have made~~ wedding plans for the past few months.

At first I was delighted, but last week I have heard something that changed my

feelings. It seems that our future daughter-in-law has ~~been deciding~~ decided to keep her

own last name after the wedding. Her reasons: First, she doesn't want to "lose her

identity." Her parents have named her 21 years ago, and she was Donna Esposito

since then. She sees no reason to change now. Second, she is a member of the

Rockland Symphony Orchestra and she performed with them for eight years.

As a result, she already became known professionally by her maiden name.

John, when I've gotten married, I didn't think of keeping my maiden name.

I have felt so proud when I became "Mrs. Smith." We named our son after my

father, but our surname showed that we three were a family.

I've been reading two articles about this trend, and I can now understand her

decision to use her maiden name professionally. But I still can't understand why

she wants to use it socially.

My husband and I tried to hide our hurt feelings, but it's been getting harder.

I want to tell her and my son what I think, but my husband says it's none of our

business.

My son didn't say anything, so we don't know how he feels. Have we been

making the right choice by keeping quiet?

HASN'T BEEN SAYING ONE WORD YET

PAST PERFECT AND PAST PERFECT PROGRESSIVE

1 SPELLING: REGULAR AND IRREGULAR PAST PARTICIPLES

Write the correct forms of the verbs.

Base Form	Past Participle
1. do	*done*
2. _____fight_____	fought
3. entertain	_____
4. cut	_____
5. tell	_____
6. _____	withdrawn
7. practice	_____
8. worry	_____
9. _____	sought
10. sweep	_____
11. quit	_____
12. lead	_____
13. _____	written
14. steal	_____
15. plan	_____
16. _____	broken
17. swim	_____
18. bet	_____
19. _____	sunk
20. forgive	_____

2 PAST PERFECT: AFFIRMATIVE AND NEGATIVE STATEMENTS

Complete the information about late-night TV talk-show host David Letterman. Use the past perfect form of the verbs in parentheses and choose between affirmative and negative.

Better Late Than Never

by Manuel Salazar

David Letterman

Late-night TV host David Letterman, often described as an "observational comic," is famous for his comments on everyday life. Even as a young child, Letterman ___had shown___ natural
1. (show)
comic abilities, entertaining family and friends. Family has always been important to Letterman. His father died when Letterman was twenty-seven. They _____ a close relationship, and Letterman
2. (enjoy)
felt the loss deeply.

After getting his degree in radio and TV broadcasting, Letterman worked as a TV announcer and radio talk-show host. Once he substituted for a television weatherman but left after only two weeks because he _____ bored and _____ to
3. (become)   4. (start)
draw objects in the clouds. He _____ even _____ disasters in cities
5. (invent)
that didn't exist. Letterman was fired. The network _____ his creative reporting.
6. (appreciate)
In 1975, Letterman left for Los Angeles, along with six TV comedy scripts he

_____. No one was interested in them. In 1977, he was hired as a writer and
7. (write)
performer on a variety show. That same year, he got divorced from his college sweetheart.

The couple _____ married for nine years.
8. (be)
Letterman was soon discovered by one of Johnny Carson's talent scouts, who

_____ him perform on the short-lived TV comedy "Mary." Carson, the "king"
9. (see)
of late-night TV, first invited Letterman to appear on his program, "The Tonight Show,"

in November 1978. Although Letterman _____ late-night TV before, he

10. (do)

quickly became Carson's most frequent guest host.

Two years later, Letterman got his own show, which went on the air at 10:00 A.M.

Although the show _____ favorable reviews, it was canceled after only eighteen

11. (get)

weeks. The ratings _____ high, perhaps because of the morning time slot.

12. (be)

In 1982, Letterman was given his own "Late Night with David Letterman" directly

following Carson's show. Later, when Carson announced his plans to retire, Letterman and

comedian Jay Leno competed to take over "The Tonight Show." By the time Carson

actually left, the struggle _____ to the point where it was dominating both

13. (grow)

entertainment and business news. Network TV _____ anything like it before.

14. (see)

When "The Tonight Show" was finally offered to Leno, Letterman changed networks,

to CBS. He _____ it clear to NBC that he would accept nothing less than the

15. (make)

job as host of "The Tonight Show." "The Late Show" plays opposite Leno's "The Tonight

Show" and so far has gotten higher ratings—giving the last laugh to Letterman, after all.

---

3 **PAST PERFECT:** *YES/NO* **QUESTIONS AND SHORT ANSWERS**

Look at David Letterman's schedule. Ask and answer questions about it.

A.M.
○   *get up*
go for jog
drive to New York City
10:30—arrive at the studio
○   *work with staff and crew*

P.M.
○   *tape evening show*
meet with producers
drive back to Connecticut
dinner
○   *watch TV*
10:30—go to bed

Source: Based on information from Caroline Latham, "Does Anyone Know the Real David Letterman?" *Cosmopolitan,* January 1987.

(continued on next page)

1. It was 11:00 A.M.

A: _____Had he gotten up_____ yet?

B: _____Yes, he had._____

2. Letterman was going for his morning jog.

A: _____ to New York yet?

B: _____

3. It was 9:00 A.M.

A: _____ at the studio by then?

B: _____

4. It was noon.

A: _____ for a jog yet?

B: _____

5. It was late afternoon.

A: _____ with his staff and crew by then?

B: _____

6. At 1:00 Letterman was still working with his staff.

A: _____ with the producers yet?

B: _____

7. At 6:00 Letterman met with the producers.

A: _____ the evening show yet?

B: _____

8. Letterman was on his way home to Connecticut.

A: _____ dinner yet?

B: _____

9. "Late Night" was on TV at 12:30 A.M.

A: _____ to bed yet?

B: _____

4 SIMPLE PAST TENSE AND PAST PERFECT IN TIME CLAUSES

Jay Leno is another late-night TV talk-show host. This timeline shows some important events in his life.

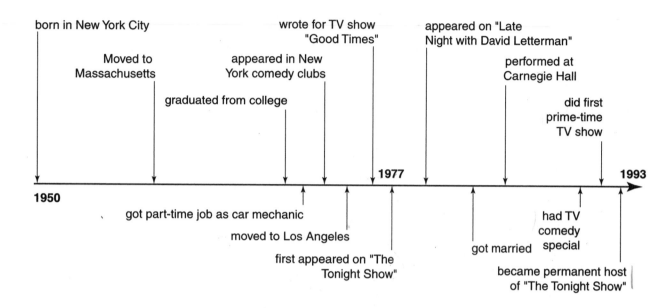

Use the timeline to determine the correct order of the events below. Then combine the phrases, using the past perfect to express the event that occurred first. Use commas when necessary.

1. moved to Massachusetts / graduated from college

By the time ___he graduated from college, he had moved to Massachusetts.___

2. appeared in New York City comedy clubs / got a part-time job as a car mechanic

Before _____

3. moved to Los Angeles / wrote for TV

_____ after _____

4. appeared on "The Tonight Show" / wrote for the TV show "Good Times"

By the time _____

5. appeared on "The Tonight Show" / appeared on "Late Night with David Letterman"

_____ before _____

6. got married / appeared on "Late Night with David Letterman"

When _____ already _____

(continued on next page)

7. did his first prime-time TV show / performed at Carnegie Hall

By the time _____

8. had a TV comedy special / did his first prime-time TV show

_____ by the time _____

9. became the permanent host of "The Tonight Show" / appeared on "The Tonight Show"

many times

_____ when _____

---

5 **PAST PERFECT PROGRESSIVE:**
AFFIRMATIVE AND NEGATIVE STATEMENTS

Read the situations. Use the past perfect progressive form of the correct verbs from the box to draw conclusions. Choose between affirmative and negative forms.

cry	do	drink	eat	interview	laugh
listen	pay	rain	tell	wash	~~watch~~

1. When I got home, Mara wasn't in the living room, but the TV was on.

_____ She had been watching _____ TV.

2. The lights were off, and none of her schoolbooks were around.

She _____ homework.

3. "The Tonight Show" was on. The audience was laughing.

Jay Leno _____ jokes.

4. The window was open, and the floor was a little wet.

It _____

5. There was half a sandwich on the coffee table.

Mara _____ the sandwich.

6. There was an unopened bottle of soda next to the sandwich.

She _____ the soda.

7. Mara entered the room. There were tears on her face.

At first I thought she _____

8. I was wrong. Mara wasn't upset.

She _____ hard at Leno's jokes.

9. There was a stack of clean plates in the kitchen sink.

She _____ dishes.

10. Mara could hear the TV from the kitchen.

She _____ to Leno's jokes from the kitchen.

11. The show was almost over. Leno was thanking one of his guests.

He _____ comedian Margaret Cho.

12. I was surprised that the show was almost over.

I _____ attention to the time.

6 PAST PERFECT PROGRESSIVE: QUESTIONS AND SHORT ANSWERS

Complete these conversations with the past perfect progressive form of the verbs in parentheses and with short answers.

1. A: Did you enjoy the show?

B: Yes. It was great to finally get to see Leno live.

A: _____Had_____ you _____been waiting_____ a long time
        (wait)

to get tickets?

B: _____. I'm from out of town, so it was difficult to get

tickets for the nights I could come.

2. A: When you came out of the theater, you had tears in your eyes.

_____ you _____?
                                              (cry)

B: _____. Those were tears of laughter!

3. A: Did you enjoy Leno's guests?

B: Yes. That Margaret Cho is really pretty funny!

A: _____ you _____ to find her
                                                        (expect)

so funny?

B: _____. I had never even heard of her before.

(continued on next page)

4. A: You two looked very serious when you walked out the door.

_____ you _____?

(argue)

B: _____. My husband thought that Leno shouldn't joke

about certain topics. I disagreed. We always have the same argument.

5. A: Cho said she had just returned to Los Angeles.

B: _____ she _____?

(travel)

A: _____. She had been on tour in Canada. She likes to

perform at college campuses.

6. A: When we got out of the theater, the ground was all wet.

B: _____ it _____ ?

(rain)

A: _____. I guess the theater owners had decided to wash the

streets while we were inside.

7 PAST PERFECT AND PAST PERFECT PROGRESSIVE

*Complete this article with the past perfect or past perfect progressive
form of the verbs in parentheses. Use the past perfect progressive when
possible.*

Queen of Comedy

by Yoon Song

Margaret Cho was born in San Francisco on December 5,

1968. Her parents _____ had left _____ Korea and

1. (leave)

_____ to the United States four

2. (immigrate)

years before. Cho grew up in San Francisco, where she

attended the High School of Performing Arts and a theater

program at San Francisco State University. By the time she

won her first comedy contest, she _____ regularly at a
                                        3. (perform)

comedy club located above her parents' bookstore. Cho _____
                                                        4. (work)

for her parents and _____ upstairs to perform during her
                             5. (go)

breaks.

    In 1992, Cho moved to Los Angeles. There she won the American Comedy Award

for Top Female Comedian. At the time, she _____ students
                                            6. (entertain)

for two years with her stand-up comedy, which she performed on college campuses.

Cho was becoming very popular.

    By the time she got her own TV comedy series, "All-American Girl," she

_____ already _____ on Arsenio
                                      7. (appear)

Hall's late-night talk show. Cho _____ a long and
                                      8. (count on)

successful show, but her series was canceled after only six months. As the first series

featuring an Asian family, it _____ a lot of controversy.
                                      9. (create)

Some people felt that the show _____ Asians accurately.
                                   10. (not represent)

Cho was very disappointed, but she _____ a lot from the
                                      11. (learn)

experience. She has continued performing at clubs and theaters and on college

campuses and has appeared on all the major late-night talk shows. When asked about

her goals, Cho says, "There's a great lack of different faces out there. I think part of

my journey has to be illustrating my experience. . . . I've gotten to a great place in

my life. I just want to do it for a long time."

UNIT

FUTURE AND FUTURE PROGRESSIVE

1 CONTRAST OF FUTURE FORMS

Read the conversations between two neighbors. Circle the most appropriate future forms.

1. **A:** Hi, Jan. What are you doing?

   B: Packing. We'll move / We're moving tomorrow.

2. **A:** Do you need any help?

   B: I could use a hand.

   A: Fine. I'll come / I'm going to come right away.

3. **A:** Do you take / Are you taking the refrigerator?

   B: No. Our new house already has one.

4. **A:** I can't reach that vase.

   B: No problem. I'm handing / I'll hand it to you.

5. **A:** Watch out! It'll fall / It's going to fall!

   B: Don't worry. I've got it.

6. **A:** You're moving / You'll move out of state, aren't you?

   B: Yes. To Boston.

7. **A:** Are you driving / Do you drive there?

   B: No. We'll fly / We're flying.

8. **A:** How are you getting / do you get to the airport?

   B: We're going to take / We take a taxi.

9. **A:** Oh, don't take a taxi. I'm driving / I'll drive you.

   B: Thank you! I hope we're having / we're going to have neighbors as

   nice as you in our new neighborhood!

2 FUTURE PROGRESSIVE: AFFIRMATIVE AND NEGATIVE STATEMENTS

Complete this article with the future progressive form of the verbs in parentheses. Choose affirmative or negative.

An Old Approach to a New Problem

Next year, Azize and Kiral Yazgan _____will be moving_____ from their
1. (move)

rented two-bedroom city apartment to a place called Glenn Commons. There they

___will be living___ in one of a row of houses facing other houses, all
2. (live)

without fences or hedges. They ___are going to park / will be parking___ in an area in back of
3. (park)

the houses. And even though there is a nice kitchen with a large window, the Yazgans

___are not going to prepare___ dinners there. Azize, Kiral, and their two children
4. (prepare)

___are going to eat___ most evening meals along with twenty other
5. (eat)

families in a common house. And they ___are going to drive___ there.
6. (drive)

They ___will be walking___ along paths and greenery.
7. (walk)

   This doesn't sound like the suburbs. What's going on? The Yazgans, along with a

growing number of other people, ___are going to move___ to one of the many
8. (move)

planned communities that are now being built around the world. Called "co-housing,"

these communities have cooperative living arrangements that avoid some of the

isolation and loneliness of suburban life.

   While the Yazgans get to know their neighbors, they ___will be___

also ___saving___ money. For starters, they ___are going to buy___
9. (save)   **10. (buy)**

a lawn mower or a washer-dryer since the community shares large equipment. And they

___will be paying___ food, utility, or child care bills as individuals either.
11. (pay)

(continued on next page)

Child care? Yes. The Yazgans _are not worrying_ anymore about what to
12. (worry)

do when one of their children has a cold and each parent is due at a business meeting in

an hour. The center _will provide_ for that.
13. (provide)

The Yazgans will, however, have some added responsibilities. For one thing, they will

have to be much more involved in their community. Even before they move in, they

will be attending monthly meetings to decide how the community is
14. (attend)

run. And several times a month they _are going to help_ to prepare the
15. (help)

dinners and _will be providing_ the child care for others. It's clearly not a
16. (provide)

lifestyle that will appeal to everyone.

Who started this new idea? Actually, the idea itself is quite old, going back to

nineteenth-century European villages. Co-housing has been used in Denmark since

1972. Even though only a few co-housing communities have been completed in Canada,

Europe, the United States, and New Zealand, we _are going to see_ more
17. (see)

and more of them in the near future as people try to improve the quality of their lives by

returning to some of the values of the past.

❸ FUTURE PROGRESSIVE: QUESTIONS AND SHORT ANSWERS

*Use the future progressive or short answers to complete these
conversations that take place at a co-housing meeting. Use negative
forms when necessary.*

1. (when / we / plant the garden?)

   A: _When will we be planting the garden?_

   B: Jack's bought the seed, so we should be ready to start this week.

2. Speaking of gardening, Martha, (you / use the lawn mower tomorrow?)

   A: _Are you using the lawn mower tomorrow?_

   B: _No, I'm not_. You can have it if you'd like.

3. You know, with more families moving in, the laundry facilities aren't adequate

anymore. (when / we / get new washers?)

A: _when we will get a new washers?_

B: The housing committee is getting information on brands and prices. They'll be

ready to report on them at the next meeting.

4. Jack, (you / go to the post office / tomorrow?)

A: _are you going to the post office tomorrow?_

B: _Yes, I am_. Can I mail something for you?

5. Eun, you and Bon-Hua are in charge of dinner Friday night. (what / you / make?)

A: _what are you making?_

B: How does vegetable soup, roast chicken, corn bread, salad, and chocolate chip

cookies sound?

6. (who / watch the kids tomorrow?)

A: _Who will be watching your kids tomorrow?_

Al was supposed to do it, but he's still sick.

B: That's no problem. I can take care of them.

7. (the entertainment committee / plan anything else in the near future?)

A: _Are the entainment committee are planning anything else in the future?_

I really enjoyed that slide show last month.

B: _Yes_. We're thinking of organizing a square dance.

8. As you know, this is my husband's and my first meeting. (we / meet every month?)

A: _____

B: _____. Meetings take place the fifteenth of every month.

9. I was just looking at my calendar. The fifteenth of next month is a Sunday. (we / meet

then?)

A: _____

B: _____. When the fifteenth falls on a weekend, we switch

the meeting to the following Monday.

4 FUTURE PROGRESSIVE OR SIMPLE PRESENT TENSE

Look at Azize and Kiral Yazgan's schedules for tomorrow. Complete the statements.

Azize

8:00 go to the post office

9:00 fax reports

10:00 have phone conference with John Smith

11:00 work on the Jansen report

12:00 lunch with Sara Neumann

1:00 bill clients

4:00 take Saril to the dentist

5:00 shop for food

7:00 pay bills

Kiral

8:00 take the car in for inspection

9:00 meet with the boss

10:00 attend the time-management seminar

11:00

12:00 lunch with Jack Allen

1:00 draft the A & W proposal

4:00 pick up the car

5:00 take Dursan to the barber

7:00 cut the grass

1. While Azize _____*goes to*_____ the post office, Kiral
   ___*will be taking the car in for inspection*___.

2. Kiral _____ his boss while Azize
   _____.

3. While Kiral _____ a time-management seminar, Azize
   _____.

4. While Azize _____ lunch with Sara Neumann, Kiral
   _____.

5. Azize _____ while Kiral _____

_____ the A & W proposal.

6. While Kiral _____ the car, Azize

_____ .

7. Azize _____ food while Kiral

_____ .

8. While Azize _____ the bills, Kiral

_____ .

5 EDITING

Read Kiral's note to Azize. Find and correct seven mistakes in the use of the future and the future progressive. The first mistake is already corrected.

> *8:00 p.m.*
>
> *Azize—*
>   'm going
> *I ~~go~~ to Jack's with the kids in a few minutes. We'll be play cards*
>
> *until 10:30 or so. While we'll play cards, Jack's daughter will be*
>
> *watching the kids.*
>
> *It will rain, so I closed all the windows.*
>
> *Don't forget to watch "ER"! It'll start at 10:00.*
>
> *I call you after the card game because by the time we get home*
>
> *you're sleeping.*
>
> *Enjoy your evening!*
>
> *Love,*
>
> *K*

FUTURE PERFECT AND
FUTURE PERFECT PROGRESSIVE

1 AFFIRMATIVE AND NEGATIVE STATEMENTS

Complete the article with the future perfect or the future perfect progressive form of the verbs in parentheses.

As of December this year, Pam and Jessica Weiner
_____will have been working_____ as personal time-management
　　　　　1. (work)
consultants for five years. Tired of disorganization at home, Pam and

Jessica developed a system that worked so well that they started

teaching it to others. By this anniversary celebration, hundreds of

people _____ the Weiners' seminars, and
　　　　　　　　2. (complete)
these efficient sisters _____ them manage
　　　　　　　　　　　3. (help)
the confusion in their personal lives.

　　"What a difference their seminars made!" exclaimed Corinne

Smith, who completed the course a few years ago. "This December,

I _____ their system for two years. I
　　　4. (use)
used to do my holiday shopping on December 23. This year, I

_____ all my gifts by November 1,
　　　5. (buy)
and I _____ them too."
　　　6. (wrap)
　　Why do we need a system? "Our lives are so complicated

that we can't remember it all," explained Pam Weiner. "A good

example is a new family in our seminar. They have two children,

they both work, but they have no system. By Monday, they

_____ the week's menu, and they
　　　7. (not plan)

_____ on a driving schedule for the week's activities.

8. (not decide)

That means that by Friday, they _____ probably

_____ for days about these things."

9. (argue)

The Metcalfs, one of many satisfied families, feel that their life has

improved a lot since they finished the seminars. "At the end of this week,

we _____ our energy arguing about who does

10. (not waste)

what in the house," Aida Metcalf told us. "And we can plan for fun activities. We

know that we _____ all the housework by Saturday,

11. (complete)

and we can make plans to go out. When we go back to work on Monday, we

_____ a good time for two days, and we'll feel

12. (have)

refreshed."

The system also works for long-range planning. "Before the seminars, our

summers were a nightmare," Aida says. "We never did the things we wanted to

do. But by the end of August this year, we _____ in

13. (participate)

our community yard sale and _____ the house. And I

14. (redecorate)

can be sure that we _____ all the preparations for our

15. (make)

September family get-together."

Children enjoy using the system, too. "I made a calendar for Corrie, our

twelve-year-old," reported Arnie Metcalf. "By the time she gets on the school

bus tomorrow morning, she _____ several chores. She

16. (do)

_____ her room, for example, and probably, she

17. (straighten)

_____ her own lunch as well."

18. (pack)

The Weiners are scheduled to appear on tomorrow's "Around Town," and this

also represents a kind of anniversary for them. "Our television appearances

started with this show," Pam Weiner told us. "As of tomorrow, we

_____ our system to televison audiences for a year."

19. (explain)

② QUESTIONS AND RESPONSES

Complete the conversations with short answers or the future perfect or future perfect progressive form of the verbs in parentheses.

1. A: I'm going shopping. 'Bye.

   B: I have to leave at two o'clock for a dentist appointment.

   _____Will_____ you ____have brought____ the car back by then?
   (bring)

   A: _____. I don't have much to buy.

2. A: Corrie, your group is singing at the fund raiser next weekend, right? By three

   o'clock, how long _____ you _____?
   (sing)

   B: About half an hour. Why?

   A: There's a rock band from the high school that wants to start at three.

3. A: This is Aida. I'm in charge of the handicrafts booth this year. How many

   of those nice dish towels _____ you _____ by
   (sew)

   Sunday? Do you know?

   B: Oh, at least twenty.

4. A: Oh, no. I forgot about carpooling today.

   B: Suppose you leave right now. How long _____ the kids

   _____ by the time you get there?
   (wait)

   A: Only about fifteen minutes. I guess that's not a big deal.

5. A: Arnie, _____ the paint _____ downstairs
   (dry)

   by the fifteenth?

   B: _____. We'd better give it until the sixteenth. Why?

   A: I want to hang the curtains.

6. A: _____ the cleaners _____ them by then?
   (deliver)

   B: _____. They promised me I'd have them on the twelfth.

7. A: Do you realize that September first is an anniversary? That's the date we moved into

   this house.

   B: How many years _____ we _____ here?
   (live)

   A: Ten. Amazing, isn't it?

3 QUESTIONS AND AFFIRMATIVE STATEMENTS

Look at the Metcalfs' calendar for August. Write questions and answers about their activities. Choose between the future perfect and the future perfect progressive.

August

Sunday	Monday	Tuesday	Wednesday	Thursday	Friday	Saturday
1 Aida walk 1/2 mi every day	**2** Arnie paint first bedroom	**3** Arnie paint second bedroom	**4** Arnie paint bathroom	**5** Aida start driving in carpool for day camp	**6**	**7**
8 Aida water garden daily	**9** Start picking vegetables daily	**10**	**11** Arnie paint downstairs	**12** - - - - - - - - - -	**13**	**14** →
15 Arnie finish painting indoors	**16** Arnie 4:00 P.M. dentist appointment	**17** Corrie pick blueberries for pies (need 3 quarts)	**18**	**19** Aida start baking pies for bake sale (agreed to bring 6 pies)	**20**	**21** Bake sale for fund raiser at Community Center
22 Aida start unpacking fall clothing	**23** - - - - - - - -	**24** →	**25** Iron and put away fall clothing	**26** Last day of carpool	**27**	**28**
29 Aida and Arnie pack for trip to Mom and Dad's	**30** - - - - - - →	**31** Travel to Mom and Dad's - - - →				

1. (how many miles / Aida / walk / by August 31?)

A: How many miles will Aida have walked by August 31?

B: She'll have walked 15 1/2 miles.

(continued on next page)

2. (how long / Aida / walk / by August 31?)

A: _____

B: _____

3. (how many rooms / Arnie / paint / by August 5?)

A: _____

B: _____

4. (how long / Arnie / paint downstairs / by August 15?)

A: _____

B: _____

5. (on August 16, / Arnie / leave / for his dentist appointment / by four o'clock?)

A: _____

B: _____

6. (Aida / unpack / all the fall clothing / by August 23?)

A: _____

B: _____

7. (how long / Aida / drive in the carpool / by August 19?)

A: _____

B: _____

8. (how many quarts of blueberries / Corrie / pick / by August 19?)

A: _____

B: _____

9. (how many pies / Aida / bake / by August 21?)

A: _____

B: _____

10. (they / finish / packing for the trip / by August 31?

A: _____

B: _____

NEGATIVE *YES/NO* QUESTIONS AND TAG QUESTIONS

UNIT 7

 1 AFFIRMATIVE AND NEGATIVE TAG QUESTIONS AND SHORT ANSWERS

A couple wants to rent an apartment. Complete their questions to the landlord. Provide short answers based on the apartment ad.

> N. Smithfield unfurn. 1 BR in owner occup. bldg., renovated kitchen w. all new appliances, incl. DW, near all transp. & shopping, $500/mo. + util., avail. for immed. occup. No pets. 555-7738

1. **A:** The rent is $500, _isn't it?_

   B: _Yes, it is._

2. **A:** The rent includes electricity, _____

   B: _____

3. **A:** It isn't furnished, _____

   B: _____

4. **A:** You've renovated the kitchen, _____

   B: _____

5. **A:** The kitchen doesn't have a dishwasher, _____

   B: _____

6. **A:** You just put in a new refrigerator, _____

   B: _____

35

(continued on next page)

7. **A:** There's a bus nearby, _____

   B: _____

8. **A:** We can't move in right away, _____

   B: _____

9. **A:** You won't allow pets, _____

   B: _____

10. **A:** You live right in the building, _____

    B: _____

2 NEGATIVE QUESTIONS AND SHORT ANSWERS

Todd is finding out information about two communities. Complete his conversation with a realtor. Use negative questions to ask about Greenwood. Use short answers based on the information in the box.

Greenwood—Community Profile

Greenwood became a town in 1782.

Schools: Greenwood High School, Greenwood Community College

Shopping: Greenwood Mall

Transportation: local public bus

Recreational Facilities: Briar State Park, Greenwood Beach (private),

Davis Baseball Stadium (planned for next year)

Cultural Opportunities: movie theaters (Greenwood Mall)

Average Rent: $678

---

1. **REALTOR:** North Smithfield has a community college.

   TODD: _Doesn't Greenwood have a community college?_

   REALTOR: _Yes, it does._

2. **REALTOR:** North Smithfield has a public beach.

   TODD: _____

   REALTOR: _____

3. **REALTOR:** There's an airport in North Smithfield.

   TODD: _____

   REALTOR: _____

4. **REALTOR:** You can see live theater in North Smithfield.

   TODD: _____

   REALTOR: _____

5. **REALTOR:** People in North Smithfield shop at the mall.

   TODD: _____

   REALTOR: _____

6. **REALTOR:** The average rent in North Smithfield is under $700.

   TODD: _____

   REALTOR: _____

7. **REALTOR:** North Smithfield has been a town for more than a hundred years.

   TODD: _____

   REALTOR: _____

8. **REALTOR:** They're going to build a baseball stadium in North Smithfield.

   TODD: _____

   REALTOR: _____

③ NEGATIVE QUESTIONS AND TAG QUESTIONS

Complete these conversations with negative questions and tag questions.
Use the correct form of the verbs in parentheses.

1. **A:** _____ Didn't _____ you _____ move _____ in last week?

a. (move)

   B: Yes. You haven't been living here very long yourself, _____ have you _____ ?

b.

   A: Oh, it's been about a year now.

   B: It _____ a nice place to live, isn't it?

c. (be)

   A: We think so.

(continued on next page)

2. A: You _____ the letter carrier this morning, have you?
   a. (see)

   B: No, why?

   A: I don't think our mail is being forwarded from our old address.

   B: _____ you _____ one of those
   b. (fill out)

   change-of-address forms?

   A: Yes. But that was almost a month ago. Our mail should be coming here by now,

   _____?
   c.

   B: I would think so.

3. A: _____ there an all night supermarket nearby?
   a. (be)

   B: Yes. It's at 10th and Walnut.

   A: Oh. I know where that is. _____ there

   _____ a restaurant there?
   b. (used to / be)

   B: That's right. It closed down last year.

   A: That's strange. It _____ there very long, had it?
   c. (be)

   B: Just about a year. The location just wasn't good for a restaurant.

4. A: The new neighbors are really friendly, _____?
   a.

   B: Yes. That reminds me. The people across the hall invited us over for coffee and cake

   on Saturday. You haven't made any plans for then, _____?
   b.

   A: Well, I was going to work on our taxes.

   B: _____ you _____ a little break?
   c. (can / take)

   A: Sure. Why not?

4 NEGATIVE QUESTIONS AND TAG QUESTIONS

The new tenants are going to visit their neighbors. They want to confirm some of the assumptions they have. Rewrite their ideas. Use negative questions or tag questions. For some sentences both types of questions are possible. Remember: The only time you can use negative questions is when you think the answer is Yes.

1. We think the people in apartment 4F have lived here a long time.

   The people in apartment 4F have lived here a long time, haven't they?

   OR

   Haven't the people in apartment 4F lived here a long time?

2. I don't think our apartment had been occupied for a while.

   Our apartment hadn't been occupied for a while, had it?

3. We believe this is a good building.

4. It seems that the owner takes good care of it.

5. It looks like he recently redid the lobby.

6. I have the impression he doesn't talk very much.

7. I don't think the rent will increase next year.

8. We don't think that there are many vacant apartments.

9. It looks like some new people will be moving into apartment 1B.

10. We have the impression that this is really a nice place to live.

8 ADDITIONS AND RESPONSES WITH *So, Too, Neither, Not either,* AND *But*

Complete the additions and responses in the following article. Choose between affirmative and negative forms.

Bringing Up Baby

by Rosa Canina

Alana Diller has a lot in common with her neighbor Haley Brown. Alana works full time, and _____ so _____ does Haley.
1.
Alana has just hired a sitter for her baby. Haley

_____ too. And they're both careful parents. Alana
2.
interviewed a lot of people before deciding on the best person for the

job. So _____ Haley.
3.

There's one important difference, however. Alana's Brendan is a

human baby, _____ Haley's Agnes isn't. Agnes is a
4.
Great Dane, a dog the size of a small pony.

Haley says, "I feel very responsible for Agnes. It's like having a

child. Alana can't leave her baby alone for ten hours every day, and

_____ can I. Both Brendan and Agnes need human
5.
contact and care during the day."

Jack Austin, owner of PetCare, agrees. "Human children are social

creatures, and so _____ pets, especially dogs. Being alone is painful
6.
for them and bad for their health too."

"Most of us think of our pets as our babies," continued Austin. "My friends who

are parents don't mind buying the best food for their babies, and I don't

_____. They want their kids to go to the best schools, and so
7.

_____ I."
8.

Schools? Aren't we carrying this comparison a little too far? "Not at all," says

Austin. "Our puppy kindergarten performs the same service for dogs that a human

kindergarten does for children. A five-year-old child will need to learn about his or her

environment, and so _____ a puppy. A child will need to develop
9.

social skills, and a puppy will _____." Austin's company even offers
10.

play dates so that shy dogs can make new friends.

"A lot of my friends think it's silly," laughed Haley, "but I _____. I
11.

have my social contacts, and _____ does Agnes. The peace of mind is
12.

worth the expense."

❷ AFFIRMATIVE OR NEGATIVE

Complete the conversation with additions and responses. Choose
between affirmative and negative forms.

A: How did you and Roger meet?

B: Well, I own a dog, and _____ *so does* _____ Roger. My dog, Agnes,
1.

and I used to walk in the park every morning, and Roger and Booboo

_____.
2.

A: So you got to know each other walking your dogs?

(continued on next page)

B: Yep. Agnes doesn't like her leash, and _____ Booboo. One

3.

morning they were both walking off the leash. Agnes started chasing a squirrel, and

_____ Booboo.

4.

A: The same squirrel?

B: Right. Roger caught Booboo, but I couldn't catch Agnes. And Roger

_____ . She's huge, you know. She ran right out of sight.

5.

A: What did you do?

B: Well, I wanted to give up and call the police, _____ Roger _____.

6.

He kept on looking for her while I held Booboo.

A: So you invited him to dinner and found out that you had a lot in common.

B: Right. I'm crazy about dogs, and _____ Roger. In fact, I've

7.

never been without one, and he _____ .

8.

A: What do the two of you have in common besides your love of animals?

B: Oh! Where should I begin? I love hiking. _____ Roger.

9.

I can't stand watching TV. _____ he. I've been thinking

10.

about learning how to skydive. _____ he.

11.

A: Don't you two disagree about anything?

B: Sure. Lots of things. He wants to move out of the city, _____ I

_____ . I love it here.

12.

❸ AFFIRMATIVE OR NEGATIVE

Look at the requirements of various pets. Then complete the sentences below with appropriate additions and responses about the pets mentioned in parentheses.

Choosing the Right Pet				
	Dogs	**Cats**	**Birds**	**Fish**
Housing	need bed	need bed	need cage	need aquarium
Food	once a day	twice a day	food always available	once or twice a day; remove uneaten food
Care and Grooming	more than 1 hour a day; need grooming	1/2 hour a day; need grooming	1/2 hour a day; no grooming	1 hour a week; no grooming
Company and Attention Your Pet Needs from You	a lot	a medium amount	a medium amount	none
Life Span	10 years or more	10 years or more	canaries: 5–10 years parrots: 60 years or more	2–10 years
Veterinary Care	yearly visits	yearly visits	when sick	when sick
Expense	medium	medium	low	low

(continued on next page)

1. Dogs need their own bed, _____*and so do cats*_____ .
   (cats)

2. Birds should have food available at all times, _____ .
   (fish)

3. Cats must have specific mealtimes, _____ .
   (dogs)

4. Birds don't require a lot of time for care, _____ .
   (fish)

5. Dogs and cats need grooming, _____ .
   (birds and fish)

6. A dog needs a lot of companionship, _____ .
   (a fish)

7. A bird can get along without much attention, _____ .
   (a fish)

8. Dogs and cats will live at least ten years, _____ .
   (some fish)

9. Parrots have a life span of more than sixty years, _____ .
   (other pets)

10. Birds don't need to see the vet regularly, _____ .
    (fish)

11. Dogs have to have a checkup every year, _____ .
    (cats)

12. Fish don't cost much to keep, _____ .
    (birds)

UNIT

GERUNDS AND INFINITIVES: REVIEW AND EXPANSION

① GERUND OR INFINITIVE

Write the verbs from the box in the correct column.
Note: Some verbs will go in both columns.

want	enjoy	forget	stop	practice	prepare
offer	need	recommend	quit	dislike	avoid
love	remember	hate	consider	decide	learn
promise	prefer	seem	give up	manage	feel like

Verb + Gerund	**Verb + Infinitive**
	want
enjoy	*forget*

2 GERUND OR INFINITIVE

Complete this article with the correct form of the verbs in parentheses.
Choose between gerunds and infinitives.

TOO ANGRY _TO REMEMBER_ THE COMMERCIALS?
1. (remember)

According to a new study, _____ violent TV shows makes it difficult
                                2. (watch)
_____ brand names or commercial messages. Violence creates anger,
  3. (recall)
and instead of _____ the commercials, viewers are attempting _____
                  4. (hear)   5. (calm)
themselves down after violent scenes. The conclusion: _____ violent
                                                          6. (sponsor)
programs may not be profitable for advertisers.

This conclusion is good news for the parents, teachers, and lawmakers who are

struggling _____ the amount of violence on U.S. television. They had a
              7. (limit)
small victory in 1997, when lawmakers and the television industry designed a TV

ratings system. Unfortunately, Congress did not ask parents _____
                                                                8. (participate)
in _____ the system, and the industry does not invite parents
     9. (create)
_____ shows before it assigns ratings. As a result, parents are still
  10. (preview)
guessing about the content of the shows their kids watch.

Why are we worrying about _____ television violence? The numbers tell
                             11. (reduce)
the story: A typical child will see 8,000 murders and 100,000 acts of violence between

the ages of three and twelve! It's impossible _____ that this input won't
                                                  12. (believe)
affect young children. In fact, researchers have noted three possible effects of

_____ this much violence:
  13. (view)
    1. Children may become less sensitive to other people's suffering.

    2. They may also become fearful of _____ with other people.
                                          14. (interact)
    3. They may be more likely _____ in a way that's harmful to others.
                                15. (behave)

Studies show that a huge majority of people want commercial TV _____
16. (produce)
more educational and informational programs. More than 75% believe in

_____ the number of hours of TV that children watch. And the American
17. (limit)
Academy of Pediatrics recommends _____ children _____ more
18. (not permit) **19. (watch)**
than one to two hours per day.

It's hard _____ why the entertainment industry resists _____
20. (understand) **21. (make)**
changes. Parents, teachers, and doctors are urging the industry _____
22. (develop)
clearer ratings and _____ violence in children's shows. In addition, violence
23. (get rid of)
seems _____ money for advertisers. Even artists in the industry are
24. (not make)
warning the industry _____ _____ change.
25. (not continue) **26. (avoid)**
The industry may choose _____ attention to the public, but it will not be
27. (not pay)
able to ignore Congress. Lawmakers want _____ the way networks market
28. (investigate)
violent shows to teenagers. They are also asking the industry _____
29. (offer)
violence-free hours, when no violent content is allowed. Hopefully, parents in the United

States will someday feel good about their children _____ the family TV.
30. (turn on)

❸ GERUND OR INFINITIVE

Complete this interview with a doctor about children and TV violence.
Use the words in the box and the correct form of the verbs in
parentheses. Choose between gerunds and infinitives.

~~shocked~~ likely fed up with used to unwilling

A: I was ____shocked____ ____to learn____ that children will see 100,000 acts of violence
1. (learn)
on television before they are twelve. I had no idea it was that bad.

B: Yes, that is an alarming statistic.

A: It also appears that the networks are _____ _____. They seem
2. (change)
pretty satisfied with things the way they are.

B: Yes, I think that they're _____ _____ all the responsibility on the
3. (put)
viewer. That's the way it's always been, and they're accustomed to it.

(continued on next page)

A: The networks may not want to change, but I know a lot of us are _____

_____ violence during family viewing times. We're really sick of it. A lot of

    4. (see)

my friends don't even turn on the cartoons anymore.

B: That's probably a good idea. Several studies show that children are more

_____ _____ others after they watch violent cartoons. It's really

    5. (hit)

quite predictable.

decide   dislike   hesitate   stop   force

A: OK. Now what can we do about this problem?

B: Well, viewers can make a big difference. First of all, we have to put a lot of pressure on

the networks and _____ them _____ shows more clearly. They'll

    6. (rate)

give in if enough viewers tell them they must.

A: What else?

B: When you see something you don't like, pick up the phone immediately. Don't wait. We

shouldn't _____ _____ the networks about material that we find

    7. (tell)

offensive. Recently a network _____ _____ a violent ad for another

    8. (run)

show right in the middle of a family sitcom. So many people complained that they

reversed that decision and _____ _____ the ad in that time slot.

    9. (show)

A: Violence bothers my kids, but they _____ _____ a show once it

    10. (turn off)

starts. They want to stick it out to the end.

dream of   forbid   permit   insist on

B: Parents have to assert their authority and _____ _____ the

    11. (change)

channel when violence appears. Sometimes they'll face a lot of resistance, but they

should be firm.

A: You know, in a lot of families, parents work until six. They can't successfully

_____ _____ certain shows. They're just not around to enforce

    12. (turn on)

the rules.

B: Help is here from the electronics industry in the form of a V-chip.

A: What exactly is a V-chip?

B: It's a chip that is built into television sets. The V-chip doesn't _____

_____ violent shows. It blocks them electronically.
    13. (tune in)

A: It sounds like something all parents _____ _____.
                                                        14. (own)

agree	advise	hesitate	keep

A: Is there anything else that you _____ parents _____?
                                                      15. (do)

B: Parents must _____ _____ with their children. They should not
                    16. (communicate)

_____ _____ their kids about their feelings, opinions, and their
    17. (ask)

activities.

A: Thank you, Doctor, for _____ _____ to us today.
                                  18. (speak)

④ OBJECTS WITH GERUNDS AND INFINITIVES

Read the conversations about watching television. Then write summary statements.

1.   **KIDS:** Can we watch "Biker Mice from Mars," Mom? Please? Just this once?

        MOM: I'm sorry, but it's just too violent. How about "Beakman's World"?

    SUMMARY: The mother didn't allow them to watch it.
                      (the mother / allow / they /watch it)

2.   **ANNIE:** Our parents just bought a V-chip.

        BEA: What's that?

    ANNIE: It's something that blocks violent shows so that we can't watch them.

    SUMMARY: _____
                    (a V-chip / interfere with / they / watch violent shows)

3.   **ROGER:** Beakman really wants viewers to send in science questions.

        CORA: I know. He keeps on telling them that their questions are great.

    SUMMARY: _____
                (Beakman / encourage / they / send in questions)

(continued on next page)

4.   **DAD:** You were having some pretty bad nightmares last night, Jennifer. I think

    you'd better stop watching those cop shows.

JENNIFER: OK, but I really love them.

SUMMARY: _____

(the father / object to / Jennifer / watch cop shows)

5. STUDENTS: We want to watch the TV news, but the reporting on adult news shows is

    really frightening.

TEACHER: Try "Nick News." It won an award for news reporting for kids.

SUMMARY: _____

(the teacher / recommend / they / watch "Nick News")

6.   **SUE:** I'll never forget that great Knicks game we watched last year.

BOB: What Knicks game?

SUE: Don't you remember? We saw it together! The Knicks beat the Rockets 91–85.

SUMMARY: _____

(Bob / remember / they / see that game)

7.   **FRED:** Does Sharif still watch "Z-Men" every Saturday?

ABU: No. We explained that it was too violent for him, and he decided not to

    watch it anymore.

SUMMARY: _____

(Sharif's parents / persuade / he / watch "Z-Men")

8.   **MOM:** Sara, it's nine o'clock. Time to turn off the TV.

SARA: Oh, Mom. Just a little longer, OK?

MOM: You know the rules. No TV after nine o'clock.

SUMMARY: _____

(the mother / insist on / Sara / turn off the TV)

9.   **AZIZA:** This is boring. What's on the other channels?

BEN: I don't know. Where's the remote control?

SUMMARY: _____

(Aziza / want / Ben / change the channel)

10.   **NICK:** Wow! This is great!

PAUL: How can you watch this stuff? It's so violent!

SUMMARY: _____

(Paul / can't understand / Nick / watch the show)

5 EDITING

Read this student's essay. Find and correct eleven mistakes in the use of gerunds and infinitives. The first mistake is already corrected.

Asoka Jayawardena

English 220

May 30

Violence on TV

                  hearing
I'm tired of ~~hear~~ that violence on TV causes violence at home, in school, and on the streets. Almost all young people watch TV, but not all of them are involved in committing crimes! In fact, very few people choose acting in violent ways. To watch TV, therefore, is not the cause.

Groups like the American Medical Society should stop to try to tell people what to watch. If we want living in a free society, it is necessary having freedom of choice. Children need learn values from their parents. It should be the parents' responsibility deciding what their child can or cannot watch. The government and other interest groups should avoid to interfere in these personal decisions. Limiting our freedom of choice is not the answer. If parents teach their children respecting life, children can enjoy to watch TV without any negative effects.

MAKE, HAVE, LET, HELP, AND GET

1 CONTRAST: MAKE, HAVE, LET, HELP, AND GET

Complete this article about math teacher Jaime Escalante by circling the correct verb.

Recipe for Success

Born in Bolivia, Jaime Escalante emigrated to the United States to follow his passion—teaching mathematics. He taught at Garfield High, an East Los Angeles high school known for its tough students and its drop-out rate of almost 55 percent. The school administration was so weak that they **let** / made gangs of students (and
1.
nonstudents) roam the halls and spray the walls with graffiti. Escalante changed all that. He <u>let / made</u> students do huge
2.
amounts of homework, take daily quizzes, and fill out daily time cards. He believed in his students' ability to succeed and would never <u>get / let</u> them drop out of class. He considered vacations a
3.
waste of time and <u>let / made</u> his students do homework during the
4.
semester break. He even planned two full mornings of classes during spring vacation. He wasn't going to <u>let / make</u> a school
5.
vacation erase what his students had learned!

Escalante often used nontraditional methods. To develop a spirit of camaraderie, he <u>got / had</u> his students
6.
to do football-like cheers before the start of class. He praised them, teased them, insulted them—anything that worked. Most of all, he <u>got / helped</u>
7.
them believe in themselves.

Then Escalante did the impossible. He <u>had / got</u> his students take the Advanced
8.
Placement calculus exam, a national test that only 2 percent of high school students take. This difficult exam gives students college credit for high school work. In preparation for the test, Escalante <u>let / made</u> his class work harder than ever.
9.
Because his students did so well on the test, and because many of them made the same kind of mistake in one of the problems, the testing company suspected them of cheating. To prove their innocence, Escalante decided to <u>get / have</u> them take the
10.
test again. To make sure that no cheating could occur, the official administering the test <u>let / made</u> them sit at desks spaced wide apart. Everyone passed, proving once
11.
and for all that even students from "disadvantaged" backgrounds could succeed.

Escalante's story became well known when film director Ramón Menéndez made the movie *Stand and Deliver*. Escalante <u>got / let</u> the actor Edward James Olmos,
12.
who plays him in the film, spend eighteen hours a day with him. Escalante, as well as movie critics and theater critics, was pleased with the results.

What makes Escalante such an effective teacher? In the words of one of his students, Escalante "really cares. He <u>let / made</u> us feel powerful, that we could do
13.
anything."

❷ AFFIRMATIVE AND NEGATIVE STATEMENTS

At the beginning of the semester, Jaime Escalante handed out a list of instructions similar to this. Read the instructions.

SUBJECT GRADE

Tests		Quizzes
A	90–100%	7
B	80–89%	6
C	70–79%	5
D	60–69%	4

TESTS (100 points each): All tests will be on *Fridays* and you must take them in class. *No make-up* tests will be given.

QUIZZES (10 points each): Almost every day and must be taken in class; *no make-up* quizzes will be given.

HOMEWORK (10 points each): All homework assignments will be collected. When turned in, the paper should have your name, period, and homeroom number. They must be written in the upper-right corner.

WORK HABITS: No late homework or make-up work will be accepted.

COOPERATION: Five tardies* = U

NOTEBOOK (possible 50 points): Each student will keep a notebook, not a pee-chee folder or any other type of loose file, in which he/she shall keep his/her work composed of two sections:
    i. Class notes (you should take notes carefully in class)
    ii. Quizzes and tests
On Fridays each student shall submit his/her notebook to the teacher for credit.

ATTENDANCE: You are expected to attend the class daily. If you are absent five (5) times during the semester, you will be referred to the Dean. If you miss three (3) tests during the semester, you may be referred to your counselor.

PLACE THIS PAPER IN YOUR NOTEBOOK
FOR A BETTER EDUCATION

—————————————
Student's Signature

—————————————
J.A. Escalante
Mathematics Teacher

* *tardies* = latenesses

(continued on next page)

Use the information from the instructions and complete these sentences about Escalante's class. Choose affirmative or negative.

1. He _____made them take_____ tests every Friday.
   (make / take)

2. He _____ make-up tests.
   (let / take)

3. He _____ quiz questions almost every day.
   (have / answer)

4. He _____ their homework assignments.
   (make / hand in)

5. He _____ their homework late.
   (let / submit)

6. He _____ their names in the upper right corner.
   (have / write)

7. He _____ late four times before giving them a grade of U.
   (let / come)

8. He _____ their notebooks every week.
   (have / submit)

9. He _____ the sheet.
   (make / sign)

10. He _____ a neatly organized notebook.
    (have / keep)

11. He _____ to the dean if they missed three tests.
    (make / go)

12. The purpose of these rules was to _____ well in the course.
    (help / do)

❸ AFFIRMATIVE AND NEGATIVE STATEMENTS

Read these short conversations, which take place in Mrs. Olinski's math class. Complete the summary sentences, using the verbs in parentheses. Choose affirmative or negative.

1. **MARTA:** Can we please take a short break?

   MRS. O.: Sure. We'll break for ten minutes.

   SUMMARY: The teacher _____let them take a break._____
   (let)

2. **MARK:** I can't solve this problem. Can you show me how to do it?

   MRS. O.: It's better if you work it out yourself.

   SUMMARY: She _____
   (make)

(continued on next page)

3. **SARA:** The answer is 5.34.

   MRS. O.: No. I'll give you one more chance to get it right. Try again.

   SUMMARY: She _____
   (make)

4. **MRS. O.:** Your homework is a mess. I'd like you to do it over.

   ROBERT: Oh, OK.

   SUMMARY: She _____
   (have)

5. **DELIA:** Can we use our calculators during the trigonometry exam?

   MRS. O.: Absolutely not.

   SUMMARY: She _____
   (let)

6. **MRS. O.:** I would really appreciate it if some of you would help clean up this classroom.

   DAVID: OK. We'll do it.

   SUMMARY: She _____
   (get)

---

4 EDITING

*Read this student's journal entry. Find and correct seven mistakes in the use of **make**, **have**, **let**, **help**, and **get**. The first mistake is already corrected.*

November 11

Mrs. Olinski made us ~~to stay~~ ^{stay} late again after class today. She wants to help us

passing our next test by giving us extra time to review in class. She won't make us

use calculators during the test. She says, "Calculators make students to forget how

to add two plus two!" She's always trying to get us use our brains instead. She has

us solve lots of homework problems, and she gets us asking lots of questions in

class. She's strict, but I think she's a good teacher. She's definitely dedicated. She

even let's us call her at home. She's certainly gotten me to learn more than I ever

did before. Now, if she could only get me to enjoy math, that would really be an

accomplishment!

U N I T

PHRASAL VERBS: REVIEW

1 PARTICLES

Complete the phrasal verbs with particles from the box.
You will use some particles more than once.

ahead	back	down	up
on	out	over	

Phrasal Verb   **Meaning**

1. catch _____on_____   *become popular*

2. cheer _____   *make someone feel happier*

3. do _____   *do again*

4. get _____   *make progress, succeed*

5. let _____   *allow to leave*

6. let _____   *disappoint*

7. look _____   *examine*

8. pick _____   *select or identify*

9. take _____   *return*

10. try _____   *use to find out if it works*

11. turn _____   *raise the volume*

12. turn _____   *lower the volume*

13. use _____   *consume*

14. write _____   *write on a piece of paper*

❷ PHRASAL VERBS

Complete the article. Choose the phrasal verb from the box that is closest in meaning to the words in parentheses. Use the correct form of the phrasal verb.

burn up	cut down	get together	give out	go back	throw away
go out	~~pay back~~	put on	put together	set up	

Starting New

Wearing new clothes, ___paying back___ debts, lighting candles—many cultures
                    1. (repay)

share similar New Year traditions. In Iran, for example, people celebrate *Now Ruz,*

or New Day, on the first day of spring. A few days before the festival, families

_____ bushes and _____ piles of wood. They set the piles on
2. (bring down by cutting)   **3. (assemble)**

fire, and before the wood _____, each family member jumps over one of
                          4. (burn completely)

the fires and says, "I give you my pale face, and I take your red one." The day before

the New Year begins, the family _____ a table in the main room with
                              5. (prepare for use)

special foods and objects, such as colored eggs, cake, and the *haft-sin,* seven objects

with names beginning with the sound "s." Everyone _____ new clothes,
                                              6. (cover the body with)

and the family _____ around the table. When the New Year begins, family
             7. (meet)

members hug each other and _____ gifts, especially to the children. For
                           8. (distribute)

the next twelve days, people visit each other, but on the thirteenth day, it is unlucky

to be inside a house, so people _____ and spend the day in parks and
                               9. (leave)

fields, where they spend the time having picnics, listening to music, and playing sports.

They don't _____ home until sunset. At the end of the day, every one
           10. (return)

"_____" bad luck by throwing wheat or lentils into a river.
 11. (discard)

❸ PHRASAL VERBS AND PRONOUN OBJECTS

Complete each conversation with phrasal verbs and pronouns.

1. **A:** We need to pick up two dozen candles for *Diwali*.

    B: I'll _____ pick them up _____ after work.

    A: While you're there, why don't you pick out some new decorations?

    B: Let's have the children _____. You know how excited they

    get about the Hindu New Year.

2. **A:** It's time for us to empty out our pockets.

    B: Why do you _____?

    A: It's a custom for the Jewish New Year. On *Rosh Hashana,* we throw away the things

    in our pockets. It's like throwing away last year's bad memories.

    B: Here's my cigarette lighter. I'd love to _____.

3. **A:** When will we set off the firecrackers for the Chinese New Year?

    B: We won't _____ until dark.

    A: How do firecrackers keep away evil spirits?

    B: The noise probably _____.

4. **A:** Are you hanging up those green streamers for Christmas?

    B: No, we're _____ for Kwanzaa, the African-American

    harvest celebration. It comes at the same time as Christmas and New Year.

    A: What is your mom setting up on the table?

    B: That's a *kinara.* We _____ to hold the Kwanzaa candles.

5. **A:** Do you usually write down your New Year's resolutions?

    B: Yes. I _____ because they're so easy to forget by

    February.

    A: This year I'd like to give up desserts.

    B: I _____ for a few months last year. I lost five pounds.

4 EDITING

Read this person's list of New Year's resolutions. Find and correct eleven mistakes in the use of phrasal verbs. The first mistake is already corrected.

New Year's Resolutions

Wake ~~out~~ ^{up} earlier. (No later than 7:30!)

Work out in the gym at least three times a week.

Lose five pounds. (Give over eating so many desserts.)

Be more conscious of the environment—

   —Don't throw down newspapers. Recycle them.

   —Save energy. Turn on the lights when I leave the

      apartment.

Straighten up my room.

   —Hang out my clothes when I take off them.

   —Put my books back where they belong.

   —Give some of my old books and clothing that I no

      longer wear away.

Don't put off doing my homework assignments. Hand in them

on time!

Read more.

Use the dictionary more. (Look over words I don't know.)

When someone calls and leaves a message, call them back

right away. Don't put off it!

Get to know my neighbors. Ask them for coffee over.

PHRASAL VERBS: SEPARABLE AND INSEPARABLE

1 PARTICLES

Complete the phrasal verbs with the correct particles.

	Phrasal Verb		**Definition**
1.	call	back 	*return a phone call*
2.	get	_____	*recover from an illness or bad situation*
3.	cross	_____	*draw a line through*
4.	call	_____	*cancel*
5.	drop	_____	*visit unexpectedly*
6.	point	_____	*indicate*
7.	keep	_____	*continue*
8.	talk	_____	*persuade*
9.	blow	_____	*explode*
10.	think	_____	*consider*
11.	throw	_____	*discard*
12.	put	_____	*return to its original place*
13.	work	_____	*solve*

❷ PHRASAL VERBS

It is said that necessity is the mother of invention. Read about some inventors and their clever solutions to everyday problems. Complete the stories with the appropriate form of the correct phrasal verbs from the boxes.

~~call on~~	call up	carry out
catch on	do over	figure out
give up	hand out	set up

1. **Edwin Cox** was a door-to-door salesman. Among the products he sold were aluminum

   pots and pans. However, the homemakers he _____*called on*_____ were not

   a.

   interested in his products, and sometimes they wouldn't

   even let him enter their homes. Cox needed to

   _____ an idea that would get

   b.

   him through the door. He knew that people were

   unhappy with the way food stuck to pans. If only he

   could find a way to combine the strength of steel wool

   and the cleaning power of soap, he might solve both their problem and his. Cox

   designed and _____ some experiments in his own kitchen.

   c.

   He dipped small, square steel-wool pads into a soapy solution and then dried them. He

   _____ this _____ again and again

   d.

   until the pad was totally filled with dried soap. He _____ the

   e.

   soap pads as free samples—just one to a customer. The pads _____,

   f.

   and soon people were _____ him _____

   g.

   to ask where they could buy more. Within a few months, Cox was able to

   _____ his door-to-door trade, and, in 1917, he

   h.

   _____ a business to produce the S.O.S.® soap pad.

   i.

bring out	catch on	come up with
end up	find out	grow up
push up	put together	turn on

2. **Josephine Cochrane** decided, in 1886, to invent a dishwashing machine. Although she

had _____ in a wealthy family and had never washed a dish

   a.

in her life, she was upset by the number of dishes broken by her household staff. Every

dinner party _____ with shattered china that took months to

   b.

replace. Cochrane _____ her machine in a woodshed

   c.

attached to her home. The machine was made up of wire compartments for plates,

saucers, and cups. The compartments were attached to a wheel that was in a large

boiler. When she _____ the

   d.

motor, the wheel turned and _____

   e.

soapy water from the bottom of the boiler. The water

then "rained down" on the dishes. When hotels and

restaurants _____ about her

   f.

invention, they started placing orders. Cochrane realized

that she had _____ a valuable

   g.

machine and she patented her invention. About thirty

years later, her company _____ a smaller model for the

   h.

average home, but it wasn't until the 1950s, when more women began working outside

the home, that the dishwasher really _____.

   i.

Source: Charles Panati, *Extraordinary Origins of Everyday Things.* New York: Harper & Row, 1987.

❸ PHRASAL VERBS AND OBJECT PRONOUNS

Complete the conversations. Use phrasal verbs and pronouns.

1. **LUIS:** I thought you were going to ask the Riveras over for dinner.

   INES: I did. I _____asked them over_____ for Friday night.

2. **LUIS:** Did you invite their son, too? He gets along well with Jimmy.

   INES: That's a good idea. He really does _____.

3. **INES:** If you run into Marta tomorrow, invite her too. She knows the Riveras.

   LUIS: I usually don't _____ on Tuesdays. If we want her

   to come, we should call.

4. **INES:** I'd like you to straighten up your room before the Riveras come over.

   JIMMY: No problem. I'll _____ as soon as I come home

   from school Friday.

5. **JIMMY:** What time do you think we'll get through with dinner? There's a really good

   movie on TV at nine o'clock.

   INES: I don't know what time we'll get through with dinner. But even if we

   _____ early, I don't think it's appropriate to turn on

   the TV while we have guests, do you?

6. **INES:** Maybe you could pick out some CDs to play during dinner.

   JIMMY: Sure. I'll _____ right now.

7. **INES:** I hope we don't run out of eggs and milk.

   JIMMY: Don't worry about milk. If we _____, I can always

   get some at the A & W.

8. **INES:** You can bring out the roast now. It's done.

   LUIS: Great. I'll _____ right away so we can eat. It smells

   great.

9. **INES:** Be careful! Don't pick up the pan without pot holders! It's hot!

   LUIS: Ow! Too late! I already _____.

10. **LUIS:** I'm going to turn down the music. It's a little too loud.

    INES: Oh, don't get up. I'll _____.

11. **LUIS:** Should I cover up the leftovers?

    INES: Uh-huh. Here's some aluminum foil. After you _____,

    you can put them in the refrigerator.

12. **LUIS:** Oh, no. I've used up the soap pads.

    INES: You haven't _____. There's another whole box under

    the sink.

13. **INES:** Could you help me put away the dishes?

    LUIS: Why don't you rest? I'll _____ for you.

14. **INES:** Don't forget to turn on the dishwasher before you go to bed.

    LUIS: I'll _____ now. That way I won't forget.

15. **INES:** Good night. I'm going to bed and try to figure out that crossword puzzle that's

    been giving me trouble.

    LUIS: Good luck! Let me know if you _____.

4 DEFINITIONS

See if you can figure out this puzzle.

ACROSS

4. Gets off (the bus)
7. Want
11. Mix up
13. Figure out
16. Opposite of *fall*
17. Leave out

DOWN

1. Pick _____ up at 5:00.
   I'll be ready then.
2. Hello
3. You and I
4. Pick up
5. Advertisements (*short form*)

ACROSS

18. Think up
19. These can run out of ink.
21. _____ it rains, it pours.
23. Call up
25. Don't go away. Please _____.
26. Street *(short form)*
27. Middle
31. Call off
32. Indefinite article
33. Professional *(short form)*
34. Maryland *(short form)*
36. What time _____ she usually show up?
38. Negative word
40. Take place
41. Put up (a building)

DOWN

6. Hands in
7. Talk over
8. Tell off
9. Take back
10. Carry on
12. Look over
14. *am, is,* _____
15. Eastern Standard Time *(short form)*
18. Drop _____ on
19. Put off
20. Come in
21. The music is loud. Please turn _____ down.
22. Pass out
24. Blow up
27. Her book _____ out last year.
28. Ends up
29. Rte.
30. Call on
31. You put a Band-Aid® on it.
35. Don't guess. Look it _____.
37. Please go _____. Don't stop.
39. Either . . . _____.

UNIT

ADJECTIVE CLAUSES WITH SUBJECT RELATIVE PRONOUNS

1 RELATIVE PRONOUNS

In many countries, people sometimes try to meet others through personal ads in magazines and newspapers. Complete these ads by circling the correct relative pronouns.

Best Friends—I'm a 28-year-old man (who) / which enjoys
1.
reading, baseball, movies, and long walks in the country. You're a
20- to 30-year-old woman who / whose interests are compatible
2.
with mine and who / whose believes that friendship is the basis
3.
of a good marriage. **7932** ✍️

Star Struck—You remind me of Kevin Costner, who / that
4.
is my favorite actor. I remind you of a movie who / that is fun
5.
and full of surprises. Won't you be my leading man as we dance
across the screen of life? **3234** ☎️

Where Are You?—35-year-old, career-oriented female
who / which relaxes at the gym and who / whose personality
6.   7.
varies from philosophical to funny, seeks male counterpart.
9534 ✍️ ☎️

Forever—Are you looking for a relationship who / which will
8.
stand the test of time? Call this 28-year-old male who / which
9.
believes in forever. **2312** ☎️

Soulmates?—The things <u>that / who</u> make me happy are
10.
chocolate cake, travel, animals, music, and you, <u>whose / who</u>
11.
ideas of a good time are similar to mine. **1294** ✍🏻

Enough Said—I want to meet a guy <u>who / whose</u> is smart
12.
enough to read, active enough to run for a bus <u>that / who</u> just
13.
left the stop, silly enough to appreciate David Letterman, and

mature enough to want a commitment. I'm a 25-year-old female

<u>who / which</u> finds meaning in building a relationship and family.
14.
6533 ✍🏻

---

2 **SUBJECT–VERB AGREEMENT**

What are the ingredients of a happy marriage? Read the results of a
study and complete the sentences with appropriate relative pronouns
and the correct form of the verbs in parentheses.

1. **Ability to Change and Accept Change**

   Successful couples are those _____*who*_____ _____*are*_____ able to adapt to
   a.   b. (be)
   changes _____ _____ within the marriage or in the other
   c.   d. (occur)
   partner. People _____ _____ happily married see themselves "as
   e.   f. (stay)
   free agents _____ _____ choices in life."
   g.   h. (make)

2. **Ability to Live with the Unchangeable**

   They can live with situations _____ _____. They accept the
   a.   b. (not change)
   knowledge that there are some conflicts _____ _____
   c.   d. (remain)
   unsolvable. This attitude relates to life in general. According to the study, "People

   _____ marriages _____ because of a crisis, such as an illness or
   e.   f. (end)
   a financial disaster, often are people _____ cannot live with the realities of
   g.
   their existence." Their only answer is to end the relationship.

(continued on next page)

3. Assumption of "Forever"

Most newlyweds believe their marriage is "forever." This is

an important belief _____ _____ the
　　　　　　　　　　　　　 a.　　　　　　　　 b. (help)

relationship survive problems.

4. Trust

In marriage, trust allows for the sense of security _____ _____
　　　　　　　　　　　　　　　　　　　　　　　　　　　　 a.　　　　　　　　 b. (make)

long and satisfying relationships possible. It is the glue _____
　　　　　　　　　　　　　　　　　　　　　　　　　　　　　　　 c.

_____ the marriage together.
　　 d. (hold)

5. Enjoying Each Other's Company

According to the study, "Although they may spend evenings quietly together in a

room, the silence _____ _____ them is the comfortable silence
　　　　　　　　　 a.　　　　　　　 b. (surround)

of two people _____ _____ they do not have to talk to feel
　　　　　　　　　　 c.　　　　　　　 d. (know)

close." They can simply enjoy being together.

6. Shared History

A marriage is a relationship _____ _____ a reality and history
　　　　　　　　　　　　　　　　 a.　　　　　　　 b. (have)

of its own. People in good marriages value their shared history and gain strength

from it. They keep it alive with family stories and photos.

7. Luck

What role does luck play? You need luck in choosing a partner _____
　　　　　　　　　　　　　　　　　　　　　　　　　　　　　　　　　　 a.

_____ the ability to change and trust and love. You need luck, too, in the
　　 b. (have)

type of family you come from. Research suggests that families _____
　　　　　　　　　　　　　　　　　　　　　　　　　　　　　　　　 c.

members _____ warm and supportive provide good preparation for
　　　　 d. (be)

future relationships. You also need luck with life itself. This is often a question of

attitude. According to the study, "Couples _____ _____
　　　　　　　　　　　　　　　　　　　　　 e.　　　　　　　 f. (consider)

themselves lucky are the ones _____ _____ luck where they are
　　　　　　　　　　　　　　　 g.　　　　　　　 h. (seize)

able to." They don't wait for luck to come to them.

Source: Francine Klagsbrun, *Married People: Staying Together in the Age of Divorce.* New York: Bantam Books, 1985.

❸ SENTENCE COMBINING

Combine these pairs of sentences using adjective clauses. Use commas when necessary.

1. I met Rebecca in 1994. Rebecca is now my wife.

    I met Rebecca, who is now my wife, in 1994.

2. She was visiting her aunt. Her aunt's apartment was right across from mine.

    _____

3. I loved Rebecca's smile. Her smile was full of warmth and good humor.

    _____

4. We shared a lot of interests. The interests brought us close together.

    _____

5. We both enjoyed ballroom dancing. Ballroom dancing was very popular then.

    _____

6. We also enjoyed playing cards with some of our friends. Our friends lived in the neighborhood.

    _____

7. Our friend Mike taught us how to ski. Mike was a professional skier.

    _____

8. We got married in a ski lodge. The ski lodge was in Vermont.

    _____

9. Our marriage has grown through the years. Our marriage means a lot to us both.

    _____

10. We have two children. The children are both in school.

    _____

11. We both have jobs. The jobs are important to us.

    _____

12. I really love Rebecca. Rebecca is not only my wife but also my best friend.

    _____

ADJECTIVE CLAUSES WITH OBJECT RELATIVE PRONOUNS OR *WHEN* AND *WHERE*

1 RELATIVE PRONOUNS AND *WHEN* AND *WHERE*: SUBJECT AND OBJECT

Complete these book dedications and acknowledgments by circling the correct words.

1.

> To my family, (which)/ that has given me my first world, and to
> **a.**
> my friends, who / whom have taught me how to appreciate the
> **b.**
> New World after all.

(Eva Hoffman, *Lost in Translation: A Life in a New Language.* New York: Penguin, 1989).

2.

> I'd like to thank everyone which / who has been in my
> **a.**
> life. But since I can't, I'll single out a few who / whose
> **b.**
> were particularly helpful to me in the writing of this
> book . . . thanks to my loving and amazingly patient
> wife, Dianne, to all our friends whom / which we
> **c.**
> couldn't see while I was mired in self-examination,
> and to my family.

(Ben Fong-Torres, *The Rice Room.* New York: Hyperion, 1994.)

3.

> My book would not have been written without the encouragement and collaboration of many people. I should like to thank my wife, <u>who / that</u> has seen little of me at home during the last
> **a.**
> few years, for her understanding. . . . I should like to thank the NASA personnel at Houston, Cape Kennedy, and Huntsville, <u>which / who</u> showed me around their magnificent scientific
> **b.**
> and technical research centers . . . all the countless men and women around the globe <u>whose / whom</u> practical help, encouragement, and conversation made this book possible.
> **c.**

(Erich Von Däniken, *Chariots of the Gods?* New York: G.P. Putnam, 1977.)

4.

> *J* ask the indulgence of the children <u>who / whose</u> may read this book for
> **a.**
> dedicating it to a grown-up. I have a serious reason: he is the best friend I have in the world. I have another reason: this grown-up understands everything, even books about children. I have a third reason: he lives in France, <u>which / where</u> he is hungry
> **b.**
> and cold. He needs cheering up. If all these reasons are not enough, I will dedicate this book to the child from <u>whom / who</u> this grown-up grew. All grown-ups were once
> **c.**
> children—although few of them remember it.

(Antoine de Saint-Exupéry, *The Little Prince.* New York: Harcourt Brace, 1943.)

5.

> *The field-work on <u>which / that</u> this book is based covers a span of fourteen years,*
> **a.**
> *1925–1939; the thinking covers the whole of my professional life, 1923–1948. . . . It is impossible to make articulate . . . the debt I owe to those hundreds of people of the Pacific Islands <u>who / whose</u> patience, tolerance of differences, faith in my goodwill, and*
> **b.**
> *eager curiosity made these studies possible. Many of the children <u>whom / which</u> I held in*
> **c.**
> *my arms and from <u>whom / whose</u> tense or relaxed behavior I learned lessons <u>who / that</u>*
> **d.** **e.**
> *could have been learned in no other way are now grown men and women; the life they live in the records of an anthropologist must always have about it a quality of wonder both to the anthropologist and to themselves. . . .*

(Margaret Mead, *Male and Female.* New York: William Morrow, 1949.)

(continued on next page)

6.

Nearly every person interviewed for this book has been given relevant portions of the manuscript to check for errors, but any mistakes remain my responsibility. Conversations and events <u>who / that</u> I did not hear or see have been reported as the
a.
participants remembered them. . . . Much has been written about the decline of American education. It is a joy to describe one place <u>where / when</u> that shaky institution
b.
has experienced an unmistakable revival. . . . I hope this book will impart some of that excitement to any <u>which / who</u> wish to set forth in the same direction as Jaime
c.
Escalante and the many other teachers in America like him.

(Jay Mathews, *Escalante: The Best Teacher in America.* New York: Henry Holt, 1988.)

7.

. . . some contributions to my work come from people I have never met and probably never will. I am grateful . . . to the citizens of the city of Portland and the county of Multnomah, Oregon, <u>which / whose</u> taxes support the Multnomah County Library,
a.
without <u>whom / whose</u> reference material this book would not have been written. I am
b.
also grateful to the archaeologists, anthropologists, and other specialists <u>who / whom</u>
c.
wrote the books from <u>which / that</u> I gathered most of this information for the setting
d.
and background of this novel. . . . There are many who helped more directly . . .
Karen Auel, <u>that / who</u> encouraged her mother more than she ever knew . . . Cathy
e.
Humble, of <u>which / whom</u> I asked the greatest favor one can ask of a friend—honest
f.
criticism—because I valued her sense of words.

(Jean M. Auel, *The Clan of the Cave Bear.* New York: Crown, 1980.)

② RELATIVE PRONOUNS AND *WHEN* AND *WHERE:* OBJECT

Complete the article about book dedications and acknowledgments. Use an appropriate relative pronoun, **when,** *or* **where,** *and the correct form of the verb in parentheses.*

To L. F., without _____whose_____ *encouragement. . .*
                           1.

Dedication and acknowledgment pages are the places _____ an author
                                                                    2.
_____ the people _____ assistance he or she _____
3. (thank)   **4.**   **5. (find)**
valuable while writing. These words of gratitude are probably the last ones

_____ the author _____ for a book, but they'll be the first ones
6.   **7. (write)**
_____ a reader _____. This fact may explain some of the problems
8.   **9. (read)**
_____ writers _____ when writing these pages. The thanks should be
10.   **11. (face)**
gracious and well written, but the task of writing them comes at the end of a long

project—a time _____ an author sometimes _____ of words.
                12.   **13. (run out)**
   In the sixteenth and seventeenth centuries, _____ rich nobles
                                                14.
_____ artists, writers were paid well for writing dedications in _____
15. (support)   **16.**
they _____ their wealthy employers. Some "authors" made a profession of
      17. (praise)
dedication writing. They traveled the countryside with fake books into _____
                                                                        18.
they _____ a new dedication at each rich family's house.
      19. (insert)
   A modern writer usually dedicates a book to a family member, friend, or colleague with

_____ he or she _____ deeply connected. The dedication page is
20.   **21. (feel)**
short and often contains only initials of the person to _____ the author
                                                         22.
_____ the work. In the acknowledgments, _____ the author
23. (dedicate)   **24.**
_____ more room, everyone from reference librarians to proofreaders is
25. (have)
thanked.

   Most writers' handbooks give authors very little help with dedications and

acknowledgments. "It's just something _____ you _____ know how
                                       26.   **27. (be supposed to)**
to handle," complains one author.

❸ RELATIVE PRONOUNS, *WHERE*, AND *WHEN*

Combine each pair of sentences, using an appropriate relative pronoun,
where, *or* **when**. *Use commas when necessary.*

1. Jean M. Auel wrote a novel. I enjoyed reading it.

   Jean M. Auel wrote a novel which I enjoyed reading.

2. *The Clan of the Cave Bear* tells the story of a clan of prehistoric people. Auel started researching the book in 1977.

   _____

3. The clan lived during the Ice Age. Glaciers covered large parts of the earth then.

   _____

4. The story takes place during a period in the Ice Age. The climate was slightly warmer then.

   _____

5. The people lived near the shores of the Black Sea. There are a lot of large caves there.

   _____

6. Bears lived in some of the caves. The clan worshiped bears.

   _____

7. The clan made their home in a large cave. Bears had lived in the cave.

   _____

8. One aspect of their lives is their technical skill. Auel describes that aspect well.

   _____

9. She learned some of the arts. Prehistoric people had practiced them.

   _____

10. In her preface, she thanks a man. She studied the art of making stone tools with him.

    _____

11. She also thanks an Arctic survival expert. She met him while she was doing research.

    _____

12. He taught her to make a snow cave on Mt. Hood. She spent one January night there.

_____

13. She went through a difficult time. She couldn't write then.

_____

14. A fiction writer inspired her to finish her book. She attended the writer's lecture.

_____

15. *The Clan of the Cave Bear* was a best-seller for a long time. Auel published it in 1980.

_____

❹ OPTIONAL DELETIONS OF RELATIVE PRONOUNS

In five of the sentences in Exercise 3, the relative pronoun can be deleted. Write the sentences below with the relative pronoun deleted.

1. ___Jean M. Auel wrote a novel I enjoyed reading._____

2. _____

3. _____

4. _____

5. _____

5 EDITING

Read this student book report. Find and correct nine mistakes in the
use of adjective clauses. The first mistake is already corrected.

For my book report, I read *The Clan of the Cave Bear* by Jean M. Auel. This

novel, ~~that~~ which is about the life of prehistoric people, took years to research. The

main character is Ayla. She is found by a wandering clan after an earthquake

kills her family. The same earthquake had destroyed the cave in which this

clan had lived, and they are searching for another home. The clan leader

wants to leave Ayla to die. She is an Other—a human which language and

culture his clan doesn't understand. However, the leader's sister Iza, whose

Ayla soon calls Mother, adopts her.

The story takes place at a time where human beings are still evolving.

Ayla is a new kind of human. Her brain, that she can use to predict and

make plans, is different from Iza's and other clan members'. Their brains are

adapted to memory, not new learning, whom they fear and distrust. At first,

Ayla brings luck to the clan. She accidentally wanders into a place where

they find a large cave, perfect for their new home. She is educated by Iza,

who's great knowledge everyone respects. The skills that Iza passes on to

Ayla include healing and magic, as well as finding food, cooking, and

sewing. However, Ayla's powers make it impossible for her to stay with the

clan. She learns to hunt, a skill where women are forbidden to practice. Her

uncle, that she loves very much, allows her to stay with the clan, but after he

dies, she loses his protection. Another earthquake, for which she is blamed,

destroys the clan's home, and she is forced to leave.

UNIT

15

MODALS AND MODAL-LIKE VERBS: REVIEW

1 FUNCTION

Read the sentences. Write the correct function.

ability	advice	necessity
prohibition	future possibility	assumption

1. _____advice_____ You ought to start your homework now.

2. _____ I have to watch "Animal World" for my science class.

3. _____ I may write a report about crocodiles.

4. _____ "Animal World" must be on now. It's 8:00.

5. _____ That can't be a log. It must be a crocodile.

6. _____ We must handle the captured animal carefully.

7. _____ You must not try this yourselves.

8. _____ That show was great. Should I type my report?

9. _____ The show might go off the air next season.

10. _____ I couldn't tape "Big Cat" last week because the VCR was broken.

2 AFFIRMATIVE AND NEGATIVE STATEMENTS

Complete this article with the correct form of the verbs in parentheses.
Choose between affirmative and negative forms.

At his sixth birthday party, Steve Irwin _____ had to be _____ the
                                    1. (have to / be)
happiest little boy in Australia. His parents had just given him the present he'd really

wanted—a ten-foot-long snake. You _____ surprised,
                                       2. (may / be)
therefore, to learn that Steve's parents were also animal lovers. In 1970, when Steve

was eight, Bob and Lyn Irwin _____ their dream—and
                                   3. (be able to / fulfill)
his—and move to rural Queensland, where they opened Australia Zoo, a reptile park.

By the following year, nine-year-old Steve _____ crocodiles
                                                4. (could / catch)
by diving into rivers—even at night! Steve's parents never said, "You

_____ on those crocodiles, son." In fact,
   5. (had better / jump)
Bob was right in there with Steve, teaching him the fine art

of crocodile wrestling.

   Today, everyone can be there with Steve by tuning in to "Crocodile Hunter," his

popular TV show. The show _____ like a serious show,
                               6. (might / sound)
but it is. Steve is very committed to protecting the crocodile. In the show, Steve

wrestles and captures crocodiles that are living too close to humans. The people are

afraid because these big crocodiles _____ them, but
                                         7. (could / harm)
Steve is afraid that people _____ the crocodiles. After
                                8. (might / shoot)
he captures a crocodile, he carefully moves it farther into the wilderness. In these

high-tech times, Steve _____ wrestling to capture the
                            9. (have to / use)
crocodiles. There are other ways. But, Steve explains, by wrestling them, he

_____ them with fewer injuries (to the crocs, that is). And
   10. (be able to / catch)
Steve believes, more than anything else, that we _____ all
                                                      11. (should / take care of)
wild animals, even the ones that _____ having us for
                                      12. (might / mind)
dinner.

3 MODALS: MEANING

Circle the correct words to complete each conversation.

1. **A:** We (might) / can't be away for a week. Is this enough food?

   B: Maybe not. Let's pack a little more in case we stay longer.

2. **A:** (Should) / Might we drive around in the nature preserve?

   B: We'd better / ('d better not.) The roads are bad. Let's take the boat with us.

3. **A:** (We've got to) / don't have to leave before dark. I don't know the way.

   B: We (can) / shouldn't leave when I finish fixing the boat engine.

4. **A:** Do you think it's going to rain?

   B: It may / (may not.) I don't see any clouds.

5. **A:** The brochure says that visitors must not / (don't have to) build fires. It's too dangerous.

   B: Then I ought to / shouldn't buy fuel for the stove so that we can cook safely.

6. **A:** This ought to / has to be the worst engine I've ever worked on.

   B: Maybe we should / can't take the canoe instead.

   A: You may / must not be right. The canoe is quieter too.

7. **A:** We'd better not / might not forget the camera this time.

   B: I know. Last year, we weren't able to / can't take pictures of that crocodile.

8. **A:** I hear the phone. Who could / should that be?

   B: It must / couldn't be the kids. I told them to call before we left.

9. **A:** You'd better / may not remind Kate to feed the dog for us.

   B: You're right. She's so busy, she should / might not remember.

10. **A:** Oh, well. We can / must always call her on the cell phone and remind her.

    B: How were we able to / did we have to survive without cell phones?

11. **A:** Mom, you've got to / 'd better not wear boots. There are snakes out there.

    B: You must not / don't have to worry. We're always careful.

12. **A:** Did I turn off the stove? I just can't / may not remember.

    B: Maybe we shouldn't / should check the house one more time.

    A: OK, but then we could / have got to leave. It's really getting late.

4 EDITING

Read this letter to Steve Irwin. Find and correct nine mistakes in the
use of present and future modals. The first mistake is already corrected.

151 Split Oak Lane
Richmond, VA 23237
January 15, 2000

Dear Mr. Irwin:

I have watched all of your shows several times, and I must ~~to be~~ *be* one of

your biggest fans. The first time I saw you stick your hand in a nest of

poisonous snakes, I might not believe my eyes. In fact, some people have

come to the conclusion that you ought to be crazy to take risks like that.

But they still don't able to stop watching! Since your show started, you

can make a lot of people interested in nature. I am one of those people.

I am a high school senior, and because of your shows, I might major in

zoology in college. I'm allowed to take general courses the first two years,

so I must not choose my major yet. One of my problems is that I'm afraid

I couldn't find a job when I graduate. What is your opinion? Will there

be a lot of jobs in this field in the next few years? My other problem is

that my parents don't want me to work with animals. They haven't

actually said, "You don't have to major in zoology," but they are very

worried. What can I to tell them? I hope you will be able to find the time

to answer this letter.

Sincerely,

An Wang

An Wang

ADVISABILITY AND OBLIGATION IN THE PAST

1 QUESTIONS AND RESPONSES; AFFIRMATIVE AND NEGATIVE STATEMENTS

Complete the article with the correct form of the words in parentheses or short answers. In the short answers, choose between affirmative and negative forms.

I __Shouldn't Have Said__ **That!**
1. (shouldn't / say)

(Or, How to Stop Fighting Losing Battles)

All families argue, but when you've just had the same argument for the tenth or hundredth time, it's time to stop and think. Why are you stuck? What __could__ you __have done__ this time to make things different? For this
2. (could / do)
week's column, we asked Dr. Iva Gripe to answer some questions that readers frequently ask. Dr. Gripe is an expert in resolving family conflicts.

Q: My husband promised to help around the house more. A week after his promise, his stuff was all over the living room again. I pointed it out, and we had an argument. __Should__ I __have let__ it pass and not said anything?
3. (Should / let)

A: __yes you should__. Real change takes much more
4.
time. After just a week, you __could have let__ it
5. (could / let)
pass. I suggest waiting thirty days before bringing up the subject again.

(continued on next page)

Q: My wife just bought a very expensive camera. I felt she _might have discussed_

_{6. (might / discuss)}

it with me first, but I didn't want to start a fight. Instead, I decided not to buy

some clothes I need. I don't feel comfortable with that decision. What

should I _have done_ instead?

_{7. (should / do)}

A: Your feelings tell you that you _shouldn't have adjusted_ to your wife's

_{8. (shouldn't / adjust)}

problem. You're right. Adjusting only makes the situation worse. Instead, you

ought to have faced her and _tried_ to find a solution

_{9. (ought to / face)}   _{10. (try)}

together. (But see the previous question—don't expect miracles right away.)

Q: Yesterday, my wife had an argument with her boss. I gave her a lot of good advice,

but she didn't take it, and I felt insulted. _Should_ I _have ignored_

_{11. (Should / ignore)}

her problem, or what?

A: _yes you should_ . Ignoring your wife wouldn't have been the

_{12.}

answer. Next time, try to find out what she wants from you. Maybe she just wants

you to listen quietly. She _ought to have told_ you, but since she

_{13. (ought to / tell)}

didn't, try asking directly.

Q: I always make out the checks and pay the bills. Last month I asked my husband to

do it because I was busy. He did, but he was angry about it. I feel that he

might have acted more pleasantly, but I didn't say anything.

_{14. (might / act)}

Should I _have complained_ ?

_{15. (Should / complain)}

A: _No, you shouldn't_ . You were right not to say anything. Remember,

_{16.}

you asked him to pay the bills, and he did. You didn't ask him to be nice about it.

Q: My husband spends every weekend in front of the TV. He ignores me and the

children, and we all feel bad about that. Last Sunday I called him a couch potato.

What's our problem? We _ought to have been able_ to solve this before now.

_{17. (ought to / be able)}

A: Sure, he <u>shouldn't have spent</u> the day in front of the TV. But
        18. (shouldn't / spend)

remember, it takes two to make a problem. For your part, you definitely

<u>shouldn't have called</u> him a name. Name-calling makes the situation
19. (shouldn't / call)

seem permanent. Instead, you <u>might have tried</u> focusing on your
                              20. (might / try)

own feelings about it. You <u>could have admitted</u> to him that his
                           21. (could / admit)

behavior makes you feel insecure and ignored, for example.

---

2 **AFFIRMATIVE AND NEGATIVE STATEMENTS**

Look at these pointers for resolving conflicts in families. Then write
sentences about each situation, using the words in parentheses and the
language from the chart.

Conflicts That Nobody Loses

Situation	Do	Don't
One of you is a saver and one is a spender. You fight about money.	• Create a budget with some "personal" money for each partner. • Treat your partner's attitudes with respect.	• Deny your purchases. • Accuse your partner of irresponsibility.
You dislike spending time with your spouse's family.	• Plan ahead and schedule time alone with each other.	• Sulk. • Pretend to be sick.
Your child won't clean up his or her room.	• Start with small tasks. • Provide containers to help organize the toys.	• Expect 100 percent change overnight. • Yell. • Give up and do it yourself.

1. When Tom's wife asked him about a new shirt, he said it wasn't new.

   <u>Tom shouldn't have denied his purchase.</u>
                        (should / deny)

2. Cora and Tom planned a budget without any spending money for either of them.

   <u>They ought to have created a budget with some pers</u>
                        (ought to / create)

(continued on next page)

3. When Cora refused to spend money on a new TV, Tom called her a skinflint.

_____

(might / treat)

4. When Tom bought a new TV anyway, Cora told him he was irresponsible.

_____

(should / accuse)

5. On Friday, Kayla and Josh hadn't decided what they were going to do on the weekend. Josh suggested visiting his parents.

_____

(should / plan)

6. By Sunday, they hadn't spent any time alone together.

_____

(could / schedule)

7. On Saturday, at Kayla's sister's house, Josh wouldn't talk to anybody.

_____

(should / sulk)

8. As they were leaving for Josh's parents' house on Sunday, Kayla said she had a headache and wanted to go home.

_____

(ought to / pretend to be sick)

9. Hakeem's room is a mess. His parents told him to clean the whole room immediately, and Hakeem's very upset.

_____

(might / start)

10. Hakeem can't decide where to put his toys.

_____

(could / provide)

11. Hakeem's father cleaned it up himself on Saturday.

_____

(should / give up / do)

12. His mother told him never to mess up his room again.

_____

(should / expect)

3 EDITING

Read this entry in a college student's journal. Find and correct nine mistakes in the use of modals that express advisability and obligation in the past. The first mistake is already corrected.

>   I think my new roommate and I have both realized our mistakes. Reggie shouldn't ~~of~~ have
> demanded the biggest room in the apartment as soon as he arrived. He ought have spoken
> to me first—after all, I've lived here longer than he has. On the other hand, I really
> shouldn't shout at him as soon as he asked me. I could have control my temper and just
> talked to him about the problem first. I felt really bad about that—until he invited friends
> over the night before I had to take a test! Then I got so angry, I couldn't sleep. He might of
> asked me first! I oughta have said something right away, but I didn't want to yell again.
> Of course, some of my habits make Reggie mad too. For example, I could've started washing
> my dishes when he moved in, but I just let them pile up in the sink. That was pretty
> gross—I definitely shouldn't have did that. But then he dumped all the dirty dishes in my
> bedroom. <u>He</u> might found a better way to tell me he was annoyed. Last week, he wanted to
> talk about our problems. As soon as we started, I realized we should have talk right away.
> Things have worked out a lot better since our discussion.

SPECULATIONS AND CONCLUSIONS ABOUT THE PAST

1 DEGREES OF PROBABILITY

Complete this high school student's notes by circling the correct words.

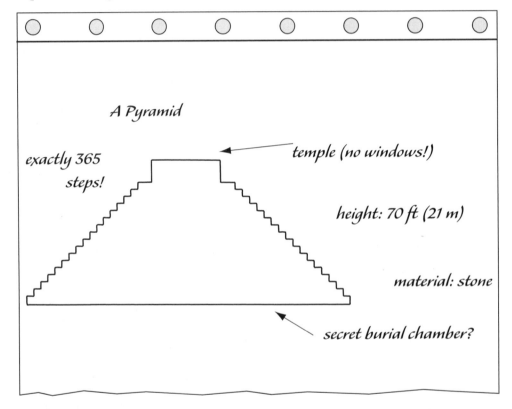

A Pyramid

exactly 365 steps!

temple (no windows!)

height: 70 ft (21 m)

material: stone

secret burial chamber?

1. It **must have** / might have taken many years to build a pyramid.

2. It **couldn't have** / might not have been easy without horses or oxen.

3. The temples **must have** / could have been very dark inside.

4. Some pyramids must have / **might have** had a secret burial chamber.

5. The Maya **must have** / could have had some knowledge of astronomy.

   Look at the number of steps!

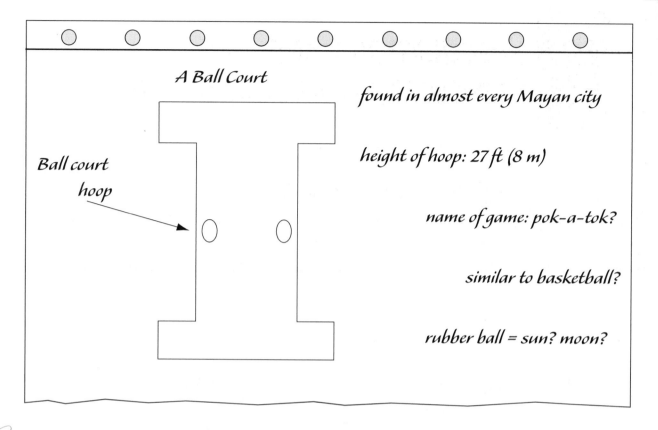

A Ball Court

found in almost every Mayan city

height of hoop: 27 ft (8 m)

name of game: pok-a-tok?

similar to basketball?

rubber ball = sun? moon?

Ball court hoop

6. The Maya <u>must have / might have</u> enjoyed this sport.

7. The name of the game <u>must have / might have</u> been *pok-a-tok*.

8. It <u>must have / may have</u> been similar to basketball.

9. The solid rubber ball <u>must have / may have</u> symbolized the sun or the moon.

10. The average Mayan man was 5 feet 1 inch (1.52 m) tall. It <u>couldn't have /</u> <u>might not have</u> been very easy to get the ball into the hoop.

11. The rules of the game were very complicated. It <u>had to have / might have</u> been difficult to score.

② AFFIRMATIVE AND NEGATIVE STATEMENTS

*Who were the ancient Maya? What happened to their advanced
civilization? Complete these speculations. Use the words in parentheses
and choose between affirmative and negative.*

1. The ancient Maya _____ must have been _____ a very intelligent people. They had
   (must / be)
   the most complex writing system in the western hemisphere and an amazingly

   accurate astronomical calendar.

2. Recently, archaeologists found four new Mayan sites in thick mountain jungle on the

   Yucatán Peninsula in Central America. Because of the thick jungle growth, the

   sites _____ easily visible.
   (must / be)

3. Archaeologists _____ very excited by the discovery. It
   (had to / feel)
   provided a lot of important information about the Maya.

4. The Maya _____ the sites between the years 700 and 900.
   (must / occupy)
   The style of the architecture and the pottery found at the sites is typical of that time.

5. The sites lie between two major population centers. The ancient residents

   _____ with these cities.
   (may / trade)

6. Archaeologists once thought the Maya _____ in the city
   (could / live)
   centers. They believed that the centers were used only for ceremonial purposes.

7. Archaeologists used to believe that the ancient Maya were very peaceful. Today,

   however, there is evidence that they _____ as peaceful as
   (may / be)
   once thought.

8. Burn marks on buildings, war images on buildings and pottery, and the

   discovery of weapons have led archaeologists to believe that the Maya

   _____ in wars.
   (must / fight)

9. Archaeologist Arthur Demarest believes that after the year 751 there was intense

   rivalry among Mayan rulers. He says, "Their ferocious competition, which exploded

   into civil war, _____ what finally triggered the society's
   (may / be)
   breakdown."

10. The rain forests _____ enough food to support the Maya.
    (might / produce)
    Archaeologists have found evidence that at some point the rain forests were almost

    destroyed.

11. The Maya _____ to other areas in search of food. That
    (could / go)
    would explain their suddenly abandoning their homes.

12. The Maya _____ enough water. There was a four-month dry
    (might / have)
    period every year.

13. Some areas _____ from overpopulation. Archaeologist
    (may / suffer)
    T. Patrick Culbert estimates that there were as many as 200 people per square

    kilometer.

14. Overpopulation _____ to hunger. Human bones show
    (could / lead)
    evidence of poor nutrition.

15. At the end, the Maya had so many problems that even a small disaster

    _____ their civilization.
    (might / destroy)

16. Culbert says the final cause of destruction "_____
    (could / be)
    something totally trivial—two bad hurricane seasons . . . or a crazy king."

Source: Michael D. Lemonick, "Secrets of the Maya," *Time*, August 9, 1993.

❸ SHORT ANSWERS

*Complete these tourists' conversations with short answers and the verbs
in parentheses.*

1. **A:** Those pyramids we saw were fascinating. Do you think they took a long time to

   build?

   B: _____ They must have _____. According to our guide, the Maya didn't have
            (must)
   horses or any other animals to carry the stone.

2. **A:** It was really hot out there today. Do you think it was more than 90 degrees?

   B: _____. Everyone was sweating.
            (must)

3. **A:** The tour guide was really informative. Do you think he studied archeology?

   B: _____. He surely knows a lot.
            (might)

(continued on next page)

4. **A:** I wonder if the guide ever heard of von Däniken's theories.

   B: _____. Von Däniken is pretty well known.
   (might)

5. **A:** I just called Sue's room, and there was no answer. Do you suppose she went out?

   B: _____. She said something about wanting to buy
   (could)
   postcards.

6. **A:** Do you think *pok-a-tok* was a rough sport?

   B: _____. The players wore thick, heavy padding for
   (must)
   protection.

7. **A:** What did you think of lunch?

   B: It was very good. Did the Maya eat tortillas, too?

   A: _____. Their main crop was corn, and archaeologists
   (must)
   have found *metates* in the ruins.

   B: *Metates?* What are those?

   A: Stones used for grinding corn into flour.

8. **A:** The guide didn't say anything about the tip we gave him. Do you think he was

   happy with it?

   B: _____. Maybe we didn't give him enough.
   (might not)

9. **A:** I don't feel well.

   B: Do you think it was something you ate?

   A: _____. I ate the exact same thing as you, and you're fine!
   (could not)

THE PASSIVE:
OVERVIEW

1 ACTIVE AND PASSIVE

Write active and passive sentences. Use **they** *in active sentences when you don't know the subject.*

1. (Active) They print the paper daily.

(Passive) _The paper is printed daily._

2. (Active) _They discovered the mistake in time._

(Passive) The mistake was discovered in time.

3. (Active) They fired Alice and Jay.

(Passive) _____

4. (Active) They delivered the copies yesterday.

(Passive) _____

5. (Active) _____

(Passive) The article was written by Al Baker.

6. (Active) _____

(Passive) New editors are frequently hired.

7. (Active) Marla Jacobson interviewed the new editor.

(Passive) _____

8. (Active) _____

(Passive) Marla was given an assignment on the Philippines.

2 PASSIVE STATEMENTS: SIMPLE PRESENT AND SIMPLE PAST TENSES

Complete these facts about the Philippines. Use the appropriate passive form of the verbs in parentheses.

1. The Philippines _____ were named _____ by the Spanish explorer Villalobos
   (name)
   in 1534.

2. The islands _____ Felipinas to honor the prince of Asturias,
   (call)
   who later became the king of Spain.

3. Today, the country _____ officially as the Republic of the
   (know)
   Philippines.

4. The nation _____ of 7,100 islands.
   (make up)

5. Only eleven of them _____ major islands.
   (consider)

6. An old legend says that the Philippines _____ when a giant
   (form)
   threw a huge mass of rock into the sea.

7. Many of the tiny islands _____ names.
   (not give)

8. The largest island _____ Luzon.
   (call)

9. The second largest island _____ Mindanao.
   (name)

3 ACTIVE OR PASSIVE

Here are some more facts about the Philippines. Choose between the active and passive form of the verbs in parentheses.

1. The Philippines _____ are located _____ in the tropics.
   (locate)

2. Most people _____ live _____ in the lowlands.
   (live)

3. Even the mountains _____.
   (inhabit)

4. Large rivers _____ on the main islands.
   (find)

5. Floods often _____ roads and bridges.
   (damage)

6. Windstorms _____ property damage and loss of life.
   (cause)

7. Long ago, most of the land _____ by forests.
   (cover)

8. Today, forests _____ over 70,000 square miles.
      (cover)

9. They _____ more than 3,000 kinds of trees.
      (contain)

10. Wild hogs _____ on most of the islands.
      (find)

11. Water buffalos _____ for cultivating the flooded rice fields.
      (use)

12. About 1,000 species of birds and 2,000 species of fish _____
      (inhabit)

   the Philippines.

---

④ THE PASSIVE: WITH OR WITHOUT AN AGENT

*Complete this information about the Philippines. Use the passive form
of the verb in the first set of parentheses. Include the agent in the second
set of parentheses only when necessary.*

1. When the Spanish explorers came to the Philippines, the islands ___were inhabited___
                                                                         (inhabit)

   ___by three groups of people___ .
      (three groups of people)

2. The Aëtas ___are believed___ to be the earliest inhabitants.
      (believe) (people)

3. Thousands of years later, the Aëtas _____ .
                                            (follow) (groups from Indonesia)

4. Today, eight languages and almost ninety dialects _____
                                                         (speak) (the Filipinos)

   in the Philippines.

5. Because they are similar, most dialects _____
                                               (understand)

   _____ .
      (speakers of other dialects)

6. In 1937, Tagalog _____ to be
                        (declare) (President Manuel Quezon)

   the official language of the Philippines.

7. By 1970, Tagalog _____ .
                        (speak) (55 percent of the Filipinos)

8. Today it _____ .
               (speak) (43 million people)

9. Tagalog belongs to the Austronesian language family, which _____
                                                                  (speak)

   _____ all across the Pacific, from Hawaii to Taiwan.
      (people)

10. English _____ for commercial and business purposes.
               (use) (people)

5 QUESTIONS AND SHORT ANSWERS

Look at the map of Bolivia.

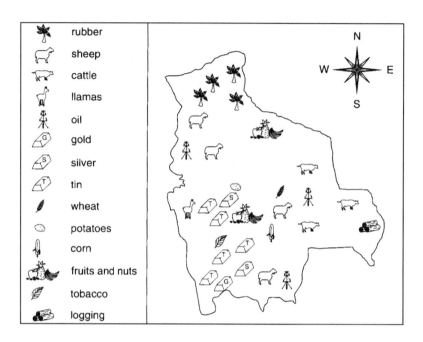

Use the passive to ask questions. Respond with short answers.

1. tin / mine / in the north?

   A: _Is tin mined in the north?_

   B: _No, it isn't._

2. What other minerals / mine?

   A: _____

   B: _____

3. Where / fruits and nuts / grow?

   A: _____

   B: _____

4. Where / logging / do?

   A: _____

   B: _____

5. What animals / raise?

    A: _____

    B: _____

6. llamas / find / in the east?

    A: _____

    B: _____

7. potatoes / grow?

    A: _____

    B: _____

8. Where / rubber / produce?

    A: _____

    B: _____

9. Where / oil / find?

    A: _____

    B: _____

10. wheat / grow / in the north?

    A: _____

    B: _____

11. cattle / raise / in the east?

    A: _____

    B: _____

19 THE PASSIVE WITH MODALS AND MODAL-LIKE EXPRESSIONS

1 ACTIVE AND PASSIVE

*Write active and passive sentences. Use **they** in active sentences when you don't know the subject.*

1. (Active) ___Many countries should build new airports soon.___

   (Passive) New airports should be built by many countries soon.

2. (Active) They will construct some new airports on islands.

   (Passive) _____

3. (Active) _____

   (Passive) Passenger facilities might be put on decks under the runways.

4. (Active) They could save a lot of space that way.

   (Passive) _____

5. (Active) _____

   (Passive) An island airport had to be built in Osaka Bay by the Japanese.

6. (Active) At the old airport, they couldn't handle all the air traffic.

   (Passive) _____

7. (Active) _____

   (Passive) Huge amounts of earth had to be moved from nearby mountains.

8. (Active) Hong Kong's new island airport will make travel safer.

   (Passive) _____

9. (Active) _____

   (Passive) The new airport can be reached easily by travelers.

10. (Active) Before, people could reach Lantau by ferry only.

    (Passive) _____

2 AFFIRMATIVE AND NEGATIVE STATEMENTS

Complete this article with the passive form of the verbs in parentheses.
Choose between affirmative and negative forms.

BRIDGING CULTURES

by Abdul Santana

While astronauts are working out cultural differences

on international space projects, people here on earth

_____ could be brought _____ closer together than ever
　　　　　1. (could / bring)

before. Engineers believe that many bodies of land, including

continents, _____ by bridges and tunnels. One of these
　　　　　2. (can / connect)

ventures has already been completed. Some others _____
　　　　　　　　　　　　　　　　　　　　　　　3. (will / start)

very soon and _____ before too long. Here's a sample of
　　　　4. (may / complete)

places that _____ by these projects:
　　　　5. (be going to / link)

England and Europe. The Chunnel between France and England, the

first of these projects, has been operating for several years. Passengers

_____ now _____ by train
　　　　　　　　　　　6. (can / carry)

under the English Channel. Unfortunately for driving enthusiasts, individual cars

_____ through the Chunnel. However, there is a tourist
　　7. (may / drive)

shuttle, and in this way, up to 180 vehicles at a time _____.
　　　　　　　　　　　　　　　　　　　　　　　8. (are able to / transport)

Asia and North America. According to engineer T.Y. Lin, small islands in the

Bering Strait _____ by a bridge carrying a railroad line, a
　　　　　　9. (could / join)

highway, and oil and gas pipelines. The bridge _____ the
　　　　　　　　　　　　　　　　　　　　10. (will / call)

International Peace Bridge.

(continued on next page)

Africa and Europe. A bridge connecting the continents of Europe and Africa

_____ probably _____ across

11. (will / build)

the Strait of Gibraltar. More than nine miles _____ by the

12. (must / bridge)

structure. New techniques _____ because the bridge will

13. (have to / develop)

be three times higher than any bridge built so far.

Thailand, Malay Peninsula. In Southeast Asia, the Trans-Thai Landbridge

_____ from the Andaman Sea to the Gulf of Thailand.

14. (will / build)

New ports and towns _____ in this project.

15. (will / include)

Italy and Sicily. Every year, 14 million people cross the Strait of Messina between

Sicily and Italy. They've been promised a bridge and highway, but this promise

_____ as quickly as people would like. Frequent

16. (might / fulfill)

earthquakes and 125-mph winds in the area mean that unfortunately some delays

_____. These problems _____,

17. (can / avoid) 18. (will / solve)

promise engineers, who propose a two-mile extension bridge that can withstand both

quakes and high winds.

---

3 QUESTIONS AND SHORT ANSWERS

Complete this interview between EuroTravel Magazine (EM) *and*
Jean-Paul David (JD). Use the words in parentheses or short answers.

EM: I'd like to ask some questions about the Chunnel. First, _____*can*_____ vehicles

_____*be driven*_____ through?

1. (can / drive)

JD: _____. Vehicles are carried on a special train called Le

2.

Shuttle.

EM: _____ the cars _____ during the trip?

3. (have to / occupy)

JD: _____. Drivers can get out and walk alongside their cars if
4.
they want.

EM: Now, what about the regular passenger train—the Eurostar? _____

tickets _____ in advance?
5. (Must / purchase)

JD: _____. Not only do you have to have a ticket, but you also
6.
need to check in at least twenty minutes before the train departs.

EM: At present, the Eurostar connects only a few cities. _____ service

_____ to include other cities?
7. (Be going to / expand)

JD: _____. There are plans to include many more cities. They
8.
are also going to add European Night Service for passengers wishing to arrive in

Paris or Brussels in time for breakfast.

EM: _____ sleeping accommodations _____ for overnight
9. (Will / offer)

departures?

JD: _____. There will be both seated and sleeping
10.
accommodations.

EM: You mentioned breakfast. _____ food _____ aboard the
11. (Can / purchase)

Eurostar?

JD: _____. There are two buffet cars offering a large selection
12.
of hot and cold food.

EM: Sounds good, thanks. This information will be appreciated by our readers.

THE PASSIVE CAUSATIVE

1 PASSIVE CAUSATIVES

Write passive causative sentences.

1. Someone does my taxes every April.

   I have my taxes done every April.

2. Someone is painting my house.

   _____

3. Someone checked my car last month.

   _____

4. Someone has just cleaned our windows.

   _____

5. Someone must do our repairs.

   _____

6. Someone is going to fix our roof.

   _____

7. Marie will cut my hair.

   _____

8. Someone should check our electric wiring.

   _____

❷ AFFIRMATIVE STATEMENTS

Complete this article about consumer fraud. Use the passive causative form of the verbs in parentheses.

Getting a Charge for Nothing

by Selma Johnson

After disasters such as the Los Angeles earthquake of 1994, consumers should be

prepared to protect themselves against dishonest businesses. As a result of damage to

their homes, families must _____*get*_____ major repairs _____*done*_____. Working
1. (get / do)

under great stress, they sometimes _____ work _____ without
2. (have / complete)

getting estimates first. Often they _____ it _____ by dishonest
3. (have / do)

electricians and other contractors because they haven't checked with the Better

Business Bureau first. The following is an example.

After the Los Angeles earthquake in 1994, many people wanted to _____

their electric wiring systems _____. One electrician told a woman that she
4. (get / test)

had to _____ her circuit breakers _____ and charged her $510 per
5. (have / replace)

breaker. The same breakers cost just $21.86 apiece in a hardware store. "Dateline," a

television news show on NBC, decided to _____ the story _____.
6. (have / investigate)

Using a hidden camera, they filmed the electrician's visit to another customer. This

customer had a broken circuit breaker, so he _____ a new circuit breaker

_____ to replace it. But the electrician told him that he should also
7. (have / install)

_____ five other circuit breakers _____. And he charged $356 per
8. (get / replace)

breaker. Furthermore, the electrician said that if the customer _____ the job

_____ immediately, there was a risk of fire. "Dateline" _____ the
9. (not have / do)

(continued on next page)

"broken" circuit breakers _____. Not only did they not need replacement,

10. (have / test)

but the electrician went on to resell the "bad" breakers to other customers.

Of course the majority of workers are honest. But how can you, the consumer, guard

against those who aren't? Here are some guidelines:

Be a smart consumer.

Do business only with service people who have good reputations. Before hiring

unknown professionals, _____ them _____ by appropriate

11. (have / check out)

agencies to see that they are properly licensed. And although the Better Business

Bureau will not make recommendations, they *will* tell you if they have received any

complaints about a company.

Use a credit card if you can.

This way, if there is any problem, you will be able to _____ payment

_____ until the issue is resolved. Your credit-card company will

12. (have / stop)

even help you try to resolve the conflict.

Get an estimate.

Always try to get an estimate, and _____ it _____ in writing.

13. (have / put)

Know where to go for help.

If you think you have been a victim of fraud, notify your state Attorney General's

Office. In many cities, newspaper and TV reporters also specialize in helping

consumers. If they can't help, you will at least have the satisfaction of _____

the problem _____.

14. (get / publicize)

❸ YES/NO AND WH– QUESTIONS

Tyler is talking to his friend Frank about his car. Complete Frank's questions. Use the passive causative.

1. **FRANK:** My old Ford's been giving me trouble lately. (Where / usually / get / your car / service?)

   <u>Where do you usually get your car serviced?</u>

   TYLER: I always go to Majestic Motors.

2. **FRANK:** (How often / get / it / do?)

   _____

   TYLER: Oh, about every 5,000 miles. In fact, I was there just yesterday.

3. **FRANK:** Really? (get / it / winterize?)

   _____

   TYLER: Well, he put antifreeze in the radiator.

4. **FRANK:** (ever / get / snow tires / put on?)

   _____

   TYLER: No, I haven't. We really don't get enough snow around here for that. But we *are* going to take a trip to Canada this winter.

5. **FRANK:** (get / snow tires / put on / for the trip?)

   _____

   TYLER: I guess it's not a bad idea.

6. **FRANK:** You bought your car in 1997. Right? (How often / get / it / check / since then?)

   _____

   TYLER: I can't say exactly. I do a lot of driving, so I've taken it in a lot.

7. **FRANK:** And you always have the work done at Majestic. (Why / get / it / do / there?)

   _____

   TYLER: The guy who owns it is a good mechanic, and I trust him. I know he'd never rip me off.

4 AFFIRMATIVE AND NEGATIVE STATEMENTS

Tyler took his car into Majestic Motors. Look at this portion of the checklist of services. Then write all the things Tyler had or didn't have done. Use the causative with **have** *or* **get**.

Majestic Motors

2680 Midlothian Tpke.
(corner of Douglas Ave.)
Paramus, OH 45455
(937) 555-3485

[✓] check tire pressure

[ ] change oil

[ ] inspect undercarriage

[✓] lubricate body and chassis

[✓] inspect air filter

[ ] replace air filter

[ ] rotate tires

[ ] adjust timing and engine speed

[✓] service automatic transmission

[✓] flush cooling system

1. He had the tire pressure checked.

2. He didn't have the oil changed.

3. _____

4. _____

5. _____

6. _____

7. _____

8. _____

9. _____

10. _____

5 EDITING

Read this letter. Find and correct nine mistakes in the use of the passive causative. The first mistake is already corrected.

Dear Petra,

We've just ~~have~~ had our furniture brought over from the apartment, and we're really excited about moving into our "new" (but very old) house. A nineteenth-century millionaire had this place build for his daughter by a builder. We were able to afford it because it's a real "fixer-upper." It needs to has a lot of work done. We've already gotten the roof fix, but we're not having the outside painting until fall. After we get repaired the plumbing, we'll paint the inside ourselves (we can't paint over those big water stains!). It sounds awful, but just wait until you see it. There's a fireplace in every bedroom—we're get the chimneys cleaned before winter. And the windows are huge. In fact, they're so large that we can't wash them ourselves, so yesterday we had done them professionally.

As you can imagine, we've both been pretty busy, but we'd love to see you. Are you brave enough to visit us?

Love,

Britta and Klaus

UNIT

FACTUAL CONDITIONALS: PRESENT

① SIMPLE PRESENT TENSE

Look at this schedule of airplane fares. Read the statements. For each statement write **That's right** *or* **That's wrong**. *If the statement is wrong, correct the* underlined *information.*

AIR ITALY SUPER BARGAIN AIRFARES Destination: Rome				
GATEWAY	**OFF SEASON***		**PEAK****	
	Round Trip	**One Way**	**Round Trip**	**One Way**
New York	$645	$375	$769	$439
Boston	645	375	769	439
Philadelphia	669	389	795	449
Washington	669	389	795	449
Chicago	709	405	829	469
Cincinnati	709	405	829	469
Atlanta	729	419	855	479

*Off Season: 4/1–5/31 and 10/1–10/31; **Peak: 6/1–9/30

1. If you leave from New York in April, you pay $375 for a <u>round-trip</u> ticket.

   That's wrong. If you leave from New York in April, you pay $375 for a
   one-way ticket.

2. If you leave from Boston in June, you pay $439 for a <u>one-way</u> ticket.

   That's right.

3. You pay <u>more</u> if you leave from Chicago than if you leave from New York.

_____

_____

4. If you travel in September, your ticket costs <u>less</u> than if you travel in October.

_____

_____

5. If you fly in May, you pay <u>peak</u>-season rates.

_____

_____

6. If you buy a one-way ticket, you pay <u>half</u> the cost of a round-trip ticket.

_____

_____

7. If you fly round trip from <u>Atlanta</u> in October, the ticket price is $729.

_____

_____

8. If you fly from Chicago, the fare is <u>the same as</u> from Cincinnati.

_____

_____

9. If you leave from <u>Boston</u>, you pay the same fare as from Philadelphia.

_____

_____

10. If you fly from Philadelphia, you pay a <u>higher</u> fare than from Chicago.

_____

_____

② IMPERATIVE AND MODALS

Read these conversations about traveling to Italy. Summarize the travel agent's advice. Use factual conditional sentences.

1. **TOURIST:** We're thinking of going to Italy.

   AGENT: You should book a flight now.

   SUMMARY: _If you're thinking of going to Italy, you should book a flight now._

   Things get booked early in the summer.

2. **TOURIST:** We're flexible.

   AGENT: Don't go in the summer.

   SUMMARY: _____

   It's very hot and crowded in the summer. Besides, the rates are higher.

3. **TOURIST:** We don't want to spend a lot of money getting around in Rome.

   AGENT: Take public transportation.

   SUMMARY: _____

   Taxis are expensive. You can get around fine with buses and trains.

4. **TOURIST:** We don't like to book hotels in advance.

   AGENT: Go to one of the Rome Provincial Tourist Offices.

   SUMMARY: _____

   They can help you find a room.

5. **TOURIST:** We prefer small hotels.

   AGENT: Stay at *pensiones.*

   SUMMARY: _____

   They're usually more intimate and personal than hotels.

6. **TOURIST:** My husband is very interested in architecture.

   AGENT: You must visit the Palazzo Ducale in Venice.

   SUMMARY: _____

   It's a gorgeous building made of pink and white marble.

7. **TOURIST:** We love opera.

   AGENT: You should attend an open-air performance in Verona's Roman Arena.

   SUMMARY: _____

   It's just a short distance from Venice.

8. **TOURIST:** I'm interested in seeing ancient ruins.

   AGENT: You might want to consider a side trip to Ostia Antica.

   SUMMARY: _____

   The ruins there are as interesting as the ones in Pompeii, and they're only a

   thirty-minute train ride from Rome.

9. **TOURIST:** We plan to take a hair dryer and an electric shaver with us.

   AGENT: Don't forget to take a transformer and an adapter.

   SUMMARY: _____

   The electricity varies considerably in Italy, and unlike in the United States

   and Canada, outlets have round holes.

10. **TOURIST:** We want to have a really good dinner our first night there.

   AGENT: You should try Sabatini's.

   SUMMARY: _____

   It's one of the most popular restaurants in Rome. I hear that the spaghetti

   with seafood is excellent.

3 SIMPLE PRESENT TENSE, IMPERATIVE, AND MODALS

Complete this article on health advice for travelers by combining the two sentences in parentheses to make a factual conditional sentence. **Keep the same order** *and decide which clause begins with* **if***. Make all necessary changes in capitalization and punctuation.*

If You Go—Go Safely

It can happen. You're miles away from home on vacation or a business trip and you feel sick. What should you do? Here are some tips from travel experts.

1. (You travel. You need to take special health precautions.)

   If you travel, you need to take special health precautions.

   A little preplanning can go a long way in making your trip a healthier one.

2. (Don't pack medication in your luggage. You plan to check your luggage on the plane.)

   Don't pack medication in your luggage if you plan to check your luggage on the plane.

   Keep it in your carry-on bags. That way, if the airline loses your luggage, you won't be left without your medicine.

3. (You should bring along copies of your prescriptions. You take prescription medication.)

   _____

   Make sure they are written in the generic (not the brand-name) form.

4. (Notify the flight attendant or train conductor. You feel sick on board a plane or train.)

   _____

   They are trained to deal with the situation.

5. (Call your own doctor. You are traveling in your own country when you feel sick.)

_____

He or she may be able to refer you to a doctor in the area.

6. (Your hotel can recommend a doctor. You need medical attention in a foreign country.)

_____

As an alternative, you can contact your embassy or consulate.

7. (You experience chest pains, weakness in an arm or leg, or shortness of breath. Get yourself to an emergency room.)

_____

These can be symptoms of a heart attack. Time is of the utmost importance.

8. (You're not sure how serious your symptoms are. Assume they are serious and take appropriate steps.)

_____

It's better to be safe than sorry. Many travelers tend to ignore symptoms when they are away from home.

9. (Don't drive to the hospital. You need to go to the emergency room.)

_____

It's easy to get lost in an unfamiliar location. Take a taxi instead.

10. (You wear glasses. Take an extra pair with you.)

_____

Many a vacation has been ruined by this lack of foresight.

_H_ave a safe trip!

FACTUAL CONDITIONALS: FUTURE

❶ *IF* AND *UNLESS*, AFFIRMATIVE AND NEGATIVE, SIMPLE PRESENT AND FUTURE

Complete the article by circling the correct words.

THE GREEN GENERATION

Who pays / **'s going to pay** the price if the current generation
         1.
continues / will continue to pollute the environment? Today's children
         2.
will foot the bill. California teenagers who figured this out have started

an organization called YES (Youth for Environmental Sanity). As one

member of YES points out, "Adults didn't learn about the environment

when they were growing up." Therefore, YES members believe that

if / unless kids depend / will depend on themselves, nothing is going
   3.   **4.**
to happen. The group is realistic but hopeful. Spokesperson Sol

Solomon states the YES philosophy in a few words: "Who says we

can't save the earth? If we save / don't save it for ourselves, nobody
                          5.
saves / 's going to save it for us." A lot of this hope is based on
   6.
teenagers' growing economic power. According to one nationwide poll,

U.S. teenagers spend about $80 billion a year. Using that power, kids'

ecology groups have told some manufacturers, "We won't buy your

products if / unless you change / will change the way you do business."
       7.   **8.**

Youngsters have forced giant food corporations such as Burger King and Star-Kist to

change. Now, <u>if / unless</u> kids <u>object / will object</u> to a product for environmental reasons,
      9.   10.

manufacturers listen.

Partly because companies want kids to buy their products, "green" advertising—

advertising that mentions a company's concern about the environment—is booming.

But environmental groups tell companies that they'd better actually solve problems and

not just spend money on advertising. "Kids are sharp," warns one spokesperson.

"They<u>'ll / won't</u> figure it out fast if manufacturers <u>will practice / practice</u> false
    11.   12.

advertising."

Source: Nancy Marx Botter, "Making a Difference," *The New York Times,* as reprinted in *Scholastic Update,* April 17, 1992, pp. 22–23.

② CONDITIONAL QUESTIONS AND RESPONSES: AFFIRMATIVE AND NEGATIVE

Archaeologists often learn about a culture by studying that culture's garbage. Complete the interview with an archaeologist of modern culture. Use the correct form of the words in parentheses or short answers.

Q: Why did you decide to specialize in garbage, Dr. Ratner?

A: I realized that the United States is in a crisis. We now spend more than

$15 billion a year to deal with our trash, and the cost is growing. If we

_____ *don't do* _____ something about our garbage, this problem
      1. (not do)

_____ out of control very soon.
      2. (grow)

Q: What exactly do you mean by a crisis? I mean, what _____
                                             3. (happen)

if we _____ as we are right now?
      4. (continue)

A: Well, for one thing, we _____ of room unless we
                              5. (run out)

_____ our ways. The dump for New York City is now
      6. (change)

(continued on next page)

twenty-five times larger than the Great Pyramid of Giza. Unless we

_____ an answer to this trash problem, our greatest
                7. (discover)

monument _____ our garbage.
                        8. (be)

Q: Is that the major problem? I mean, _____ we

_____ resolve today's garbage crisis if we just
                9. (be able to)

_____ a place to put all the trash we create?
                10. (find)

A: _____. Space is only one of the problems. These landfills
                        11.

leak pollutants into the ground. We _____ our groundwater
                                            12. (pollute)

unless we _____ this leakage. In fact, this has already
                    13. (control)

started to happen.

Q: You're studying the contents of a landfill now. If you _____
                                                                    14. (find out)

what's in there, _____ that _____
                                                                15. (help)

officials plan solutions?

A: _____. It'll help a lot. They _____
                16.   17. (not make)

the right decisions unless we _____ good information.
                                        18. (provide)

People often have mistaken ideas about what's in a landfill and what happens to it. For

example, a lot of people think 30 percent of our trash comes from fast-food packaging.

Q: You mean it doesn't?

A: Uh-uh. Fast-food packaging is only about one-quarter of 1 percent. But if we

_____ that plastic cups are the "bad guys," we
                19. (believe)

_____ them with something a lot worse.
                20. (replace)

Q: What could be worse?

A: Paper cups. They take up just as much room, and you can't recycle them.

You _____ the pollution problem if you
　　　　 21. (not reduce)

_____ paper instead of plastic.
22. (throw away)

Q: But paper breaks down, right?

A: It breaks down, but not very quickly. We often find forty-year-old newspapers that we

can still read. Reducing *all* waste is our only answer.

Q: Many people find recycling complicated. _____ people

actually _____ if they _____
　　　　　 23. (cooperate)　　　　　　　　　 **24. (have to)**
sort their trash instead of just dumping it?

A: There's no doubt that if wastefulness _____ expensive, people
　　　　　　　　　　　　　　　 25. (become)

_____. For example, if we _____
26. (recycle)　　　　　　　　　　　　　　　 **27. (charge)**
consumers more for garbage disposal, they _____ their
　　　　　　　　　　　　　　　 28. (reduce)

trash. Seattle has increased recycling by more than 40 percent by charging more for

garbage pickup.

Q: What _____ we _____ with all
　　　　　　　　　　　　　　　　 29. (do)
the plastic milk jugs if people in our city _____ to recycle
　　　　　　　　　　　　　 30. (begin)
more?

A: We can reuse up to 90 percent of our waste. One famous clothing manufacturer is

making very attractive coats from recycled plastics right now.

Source: William J. Rathje, "Once and Future Landfills," *National Geographic,* May 1991, pp. 116–134.

❸ SENTENCE COMBINING WITH *IF* AND *UNLESS*

Write factual conditional sentences with the future. Use the words in parentheses and **if** *or* **unless**. ***Keep the same order*** *as the items in parentheses, and decide where to place* **if** *or* **unless**.

Behind the Seams at

ECOCHIC

1. (you / think all clothes are the same) (you / be / surprised by ECOCHIC)

   If you think all clothes are the same, you'll be surprised by ECOCHIC.

2. At our factories, we are careful to use nonpolluting methods of production. (you / feel / good about how our clothes are made) (you / care about the environment)

   _____

3. We make everything from recycled plastics.

   (you / not add to landfill problems) (you / choose our clothes)

   _____

4. (price / matter to you) (our low prices / please / you)

   _____

5. (you / buy now) (we / contribute part of our profit to YES)

   _____

6. But ECOCHIC clothes aren't only about the environment.

   (you / want to look good) (you / love the styling and colors in our new spring collection)

   _____

7. Why are we telling you all this? The reason is simple:

   (you / know the facts) (you / not / make the right choice)

   _____

UNREAL CONDITIONALS: PRESENT

1 CONDITIONALS: AFFIRMATIVE AND NEGATIVE

Complete the fairy tale. Use the correct form of the verbs in parentheses.

Stone Soup

$\mathcal{O}$nce upon a time, there were three soldiers.
They were on their way home from the wars,
and they were very hungry and very tired.

"I wish we _____had_____ something good to eat," said the first
        1. (have)
soldier.

"And I wish we _____ a bed to sleep in," said the second.
                2. (have)

"I wish those things _____ possible," said the third. "But
                  3. (be)
they are not. We must march on until we reach home."

119

(continued on next page)

So on they marched. Suddenly they came to a village. The villagers saw them

coming. They knew that soldiers are always hungry. But the villagers didn't have

much food. They worried that if they _____ food to the soldiers, then they
                                        4. (offer)

themselves _____ that night. So they decided to hide all their food.
                  5. (not eat)

The three soldiers went to the first house. "Could you give us something to eat and

a place to sleep?"

"We _____ glad to give you food if we _____ any. But we don't.
              6. (be)   **7. (have)**

And we _____ gladly _____ you space to sleep, if we
                              8. (give)

_____ all of it ourselves. But all our beds are full."
    9. (not need)

And so it went with all the villagers. Everyone had a good excuse.

"We gave all our food to the soldiers who came before you."

"Our father's sick. We _____ you food if he _____ sick."
                          10. (offer)   **11. (not be)**

"The harvest was bad, and we need the grain for cattle feed. If we _____
                                                          12. (not need)

the grain, we _____ it with you."
        13. (share)

The soldiers thought, and then they said, "We wish you _____ us
                                                  14. (can / offer)

something to eat, but since you can't—we'll have to make stone soup."

"Stone soup?" The villagers had never heard of it before.

"First, we'll need a large pot," said the soldiers.

That was no problem. The villagers brought them the largest pot they could find.

"Now we need water to fill it and a fire to cook with."

The villagers brought buckets of water and built a fire in the village square.

"Now we need three round, smooth stones."

That, too, was no problem at all. The villagers brought them, and the soldiers

dropped them into the pot.

The soldiers stirred the pot and added some salt and pepper (all good soups have

salt and pepper).

"Stones like these usually make a very fine soup, but if we _____ some

15. (have)
carrots, it _____ a lot better," they said.

16. (taste)

"I think I can find a carrot!" said one of the villagers. She ran home and got all the

carrots she had hidden from the soldiers.

"This soup _____ so much better if we _____ some cabbage in

17. (taste)   18. (put)
it," said the soldiers as they sliced the carrots. "We wish you _____ some

19. (have)
cabbage. It's a shame that you don't."

"Let me see if I can find one," said another villager. She went home and came back

with three cabbages that she had hidden from the soldiers.

"If we _____ a little beef and a few potatoes, this soup _____

20. (add)   21. (be)
good enough for a rich man's table."

No sooner said than done. The villagers ran to get the hidden food.

Just imagine! A rich man's soup—and all from just a few stones!

The soldiers stirred and sighed, "If we _____ in a little barley and a cup

22. (stir)
of milk, this soup _____ fit for the king himself."

23. (be)

The villagers were really impressed. The soldiers knew the king! They wished *they*

_____ the king!

24. (know)

The villagers brought their hidden barley and milk to the soldiers, who stirred the

ingredients into the pot.

Finally the soup was ready. Tables were set up in the square and torches were lit.

The soup was delicious. Fit for a king. But the villagers said to themselves, "If a king

_____ this soup, he _____ bread, and a roast, and some cider to

25. (eat)   26. (require)
go with it, wouldn't he?"

Before not too long, everyone sat down to enjoy a great feast of roast, bread, cider,

and soup. Never before had they tasted such delicious soup. And imagine—

it was made just from stones!

❷ *WISH:* AFFIRMATIVE AND NEGATIVE STATEMENTS

Rewrite the villagers' complaints as wishes.

1. We don't have enough food.

   We wish we had enough food.

2. The soldiers want our food.

3. We have to hide our food from them.

4. We need all our grain to feed the cows.

5. All our beds are full.

6. There isn't enough room for the soldiers.

7. We don't know the king.

8. We don't have a larger soup pot.

9. We can't have stone soup every day.

❸ CONDITIONALS: AFFIRMATIVE AND NEGATIVE

Rewrite these excuses using the present unreal conditional.

1. We don't have food. That's why we can't feed the soldiers.

   If we had food, we could feed the soldiers.

2. I don't have potatoes. That's why I'm not going to make potato soup.

3. My apartment is small. That's why I don't invite people over.

_____

4. Steak is expensive. That's why we don't eat it.

_____

5. My daughter is sick. That's why I can't go to work.

_____

6. I have bad eyesight. That's why I don't join the army.

_____

7. The soup doesn't have seasoning in it. That's why it tastes so bland.

_____

8. I always hide my money. That's why I'm not able to find it now.

_____

9. I'm not rich. That's why I don't take vacations.

_____

10. I don't have the recipe. That's why I don't make stone soup.

_____

4 GIVING ADVICE WITH *IF I WERE YOU* . . .

1. A: I don't know how to cook.

   B: _____If I were you, I'd learn how to cook._____
                              (learn)
    It's an important skill to have.

2. A: I've never read a fairy tale.

   B: _____
                              (read)
    They're a lot of fun.

3. A: I've never tried cabbage soup.

   B: _____
                              (try)
    It's delicious, and it's healthy.

(continued on next page)

4. A: This soup tastes bland. Where's the salt?

B: ~~This soup tastes bland I wis~~
(not add)

Put some pepper in, instead.

5. A: I'm going to ask for a raise.

B: _____
(not ask)

You've only worked there a month.

6. A: *Rambo VI* is playing at the Cineplex. My daughter loves going to the movies.

B: _____
(not take)

It's very violent.

7. A: My landlord just raised the rent again.

B: _____
(move)

You can find a nice apartment for much less.

8. A: I'm exhausted, and I have no idea what to make for dinner.

B: _____
(eat out)

The place across the street has good food, and it's not expensive.

---

⑤ *YES/NO* AND *WH–* QUESTIONS

Several scouts are sitting around a campfire. Complete their questions with the words below and the present unreal conditional.

1. What / we / do / if / we / can't find the way back?

   What would we do if we couldn't find the way back?

2. Who / look for us / if / we / get lost?

   _____

3. Where / we / go / if / it / start to rain?

   _____

4. you / be afraid / if / we / see a bear?

   _____

5. If / you / hear a loud growl / you / be scared?

_____

6. What / you / do / if / you / be in my place?

_____

7. What / we / do / if / we / run out of food?

_____

8. If / we / not have any more food / we / make stone soup?

_____

6 **EDITING**

Read this scout's journal entry. Find and correct nine mistakes in the use of present unreal conditionals. The first mistake is already corrected.

> 11:00 P.M., June 11
>
> Somewhere in the forest
>
>   It's 11:00 P.M. and I'm still awake. I wish I ~~was~~ _were_ home. If I would be home, I would be asleep by now! But here I am in the middle of nowhere. My sleeping bag is really uncomfortable. If I were more comfortable, I will be able to sleep. What do my friends think if they could see me now?
>
>   I'm cold, tired, and hungry. I wish I have something to eat. But all the food is locked up in the van, and everyone else is sound asleep. If I would have a book, I would read, but I didn't bring any books. Tonight, as we sat around the campfire, someone read a story called "Stone Soup." I'm so hungry that even stone soup sounds good to me. If I know the recipe, I made it.
>
>   Well, I'm getting tired of holding this flashlight (I wish I would have a regular lamp!), so I think I'll try to fall asleep.

24 UNREAL CONDITIONALS: PAST

1 AFFIRMATIVE AND NEGATIVE STATEMENTS

Complete this article about Walt Disney with the correct form of the verbs in parentheses.

$\mathcal{W}$alt $\mathcal{D}$isney had a difficult childhood, but he transformed his hardships into magic. Looking back, one can see the seeds of Disney's imagination in those early experiences.

It's even possible that Disney ___**wouldn't have created**___ his many
                                  1. (not create)

magical worlds if his early years _____
                                              2. (be)

happier.

   Disney's father, Elias Disney, had had dreams too, but they never

came true. After a business failure in Chicago, the Disneys

moved to a farm in Missouri. If his two oldest brothers

_____ farmwork more enjoyable, Walt
           3. (find)

Disney's childhood _____ easier. However,
                              4. (be)

the oldest brothers soon returned to Chicago, and six-year-old Walt

and his brother Roy were left to do the farm chores. Like the

witch in *Snow White*, the Disneys sold apples door to door when

they needed money. In time, Roy found jobs off the farm. Walt

_____ never _____
                                              5. (see)

a carnival or _____ a toy if Roy
                    6. (own)

_____ extra cash.
        7. (not earn)

Once, when Walt was seven, he painted large animals on the walls of the farmhouse.

His father punished him severely, but others encouraged his talent. Some people

believe that if the local physician, "Doc" Sherwood, _____

                                                            8. (not pay)

him a quarter for his drawing of Doc's horse, Rupert, or if his Aunt Margaret

_____ him a gift of drawing paper and crayons, Disney's
         9. (not give)

genius _____ Elias's harsh treatment.
         10. (not survive)

    In 1910, when Walt was nine, Elias sold the farm and bought a newspaper

route in Kansas City, Missouri. For six years, Walt started work at 3:30 every

morning. He sometimes fell asleep in the warm halls of apartment buildings

or dozed over a toy on a family's porch while he was delivering newspapers. If he

_____ more sleep during this period, he probably
         11. (get)

_____ more attention to his lessons. But under the
         12. (pay)

circumstances, he didn't have much success at school.

    If he _____ Walter Pfeiffer, Disney's Kansas City boyhood
            13. (not meet)

_____ completely joyless. Pfeiffer's family enjoyed singing
         14. (be)

and telling jokes, and they introduced Walt to vaudeville theater. "The Two Walts" even

put together their own show when they were thirteen. Disney's strict parents

_____ if they _____ Walt was
         15. (disapprove)   **16. (know)**

acting in vaudeville, so Walt used to sneak out through his bedroom window to go to

the theater to perform.

    When Disney was fourteen, his father gave him permission to attend Saturday

classes at the Kansas City Art Institute. If Elias _____,
                           17. (not agree)

Walt _____ longer to find his vocation, but he was already
         18. (take)

dreaming of becoming a cartoonist. He overcame great obstacles in his career, but once

he had studied at the Institute, he never lost his determination to make his imagined

worlds real.

Source: Maxine P. Fisher, *Walt Disney.* New York: Franklin Watts, 1988.

2 PAST CONDITIONAL WITH *WISH*

Disney's most popular movie was Mary Poppins. *Based on a book by
P. L. Travers, the movie tells the story of a wonderful nursemaid who
comes to take care of Jane and Michael Banks. Rewrite each sentence
with* **wish**.

1. **MRS. BANKS:** Our nursemaid, Katie, left. She didn't give me any warning.

   I wish our nursemaid, Katie, hadn't left.

   I wish she had given me some warning.

2. **MR. AND MRS. BANKS:** Mary Poppins, the new nursemaid, demanded two days off a month. She was so stubborn about it.

   _____

   _____

3. **BERT THE MATCH-MAN** (who drew pictures on the sidewalk for money): I didn't make any money for my pictures today. I couldn't take Mary Poppins out for tea.

   _____

   _____

4. **JANE AND MICHAEL BANKS:** Mary Poppins took her day off today. She went on a magical journey without us.

   _____

   _____

5. **MARY POPPINS:** I took the children to visit my Uncle Albert on his birthday. Albert filled up with laughing gas. He floated on the ceiling.

   _____

   _____

6. **MICHAEL:** I stole Mary Poppins's magic compass tonight. Those giant creatures from the four corners of the world frightened me.

   _____

   _____

7. **THE BANKS FAMILY:** Mary Poppins didn't want to stay forever. She left with the West Wind last night.

   _____

   _____

3 AFFIRMATIVE AND NEGATIVE STATEMENTS

Using the words in parentheses, combine each pair of sentences into one past unreal conditional sentence.

1. Disney lived on a farm. He drew wonderful cartoon animals. (might)

   If Disney hadn't lived on a farm, he might not have drawn wonderful cartoon animals.

2. He sold candy to train passengers as a boy. He loved model trains as an adult. (might)

   _____

3. He didn't join the army in World War I. He was too young. (would)

   _____

4. His friend Ub helped him buy a suit. Disney, who was shy, met his fiancée's parents. (could)

   _____

5. Disney didn't own the rights to his first cartoon characters. His distributor cheated him. (would)

   _____

6. His art lessons meant a lot to Disney. He paid for lessons for Disney Studio artists. (would)

   _____

7. A bank loaned Disney $1.5 million. He made *Snow White and the Seven Dwarfs*. (could)

   _____

8. The movie succeeded. The bank didn't take Disney's studio, the film, and Disney's home. (would)

   _____

9. Disney died in 1966. He didn't see the opening of the EPCOT Center in Florida. (would)

   _____

10. He was a genius. He overcame his unhappy childhood. (might)

    _____

Source: Maxine P. Fisher, *Walt Disney.* New York: Franklin Watts, 1988.

4 **QUESTIONS AND RESPONSES**

Complete the article with the correct form of the verbs in parentheses or short answers.

The Second Time Around . . .

Our readers have shared some problems and questions related to their first trip to Disney World. First-time visitors can use their experience and have more fun the first time around.

We visited Disney World for the first time last April, during spring break. It was packed! I think we spent most of our time waiting in lines. Is it always like this?

_____Would_____ we ___have avoided___ crowds if we _____had visited_____
            1. (avoid)   **2. (visit)**

at another time?—**Fred and Betty Ruddle, Flint, Michigan**

_____Yes, you would have_____. *Spring break is one of the most crowded times*
            3.
(along with the Christmas holiday season and the weekend of Washington's Birthday).
Next time, go between Thanksgiving and Christmas or between January 4 and the middle
of February.

****

We bought tickets to the park at our hotel (not a Disney hotel), and they were expensive. How much _____ we _____ if we
                                                                          4. (save)
_____ them at a Disney hotel?—**K. Lewis, Denver, Colorado**
            5. (buy)

Up to 10 percent at a Disney store or hotel. You can also save by buying in advance,
by mail.

****

We visited Magic Kingdom first, and that was the end of the trip for our daughter—she never wanted to leave. She really couldn't appreciate EPCOT, which we visited

next and which fascinated us. If you _____ with a small child, where

6. (go)

_____ you _____ first?—**V. Luvik, Miami, Florida**

7. (go)

I suggest that families see EPCOT first, then MGM, and finally Magic Kingdom, which is fun for both adults and children.

****

We stayed at a hotel inside the park because we wanted to be close to everything. It was very expensive, and we wonder if that was the right choice.

_____ we _____ travel a long

8. (have to)

way to get to the park if we _____ inside the park?

9. (stay)

—**P. James, San Juan, Puerto Rico**

_____. *In fact, some of the hotels outside the park are*

10.

actually closer to Magic Kingdom than some hotels inside the park, and they're from 40 to 60 percent cheaper.

****

Our son was studying pirates at school, so our first day at Disney World we raced over to Pirates of the Caribbean. It was closed for repairs. If we

_____ ahead, _____ they

11. (call)

_____ us it was closed?—**J. Méndez, Syracuse, New York**

12. (tell)

_____. *In fact, it's always a good idea to call and find out*

13.

if any rides are closed.

****

On our first trip, we were never sure what to do next, and we spent a lot of time just waiting. My husband blames the park, but I think it could have been fun. If we

_____ more, _____ we

14. (plan)

_____ our trip?—**D. King, Dayton, Ohio**

15. (enjoy)

_____. *There's so much to see that visitors can get*

16.

overwhelmed. To get the best value for your money, plan each day ahead of time.

Source: *Bottom Line Personal,* June 15, 1993. From an interview with Bob Sehlinger, author of *The Unofficial Guide to Walt Disney World and EPCOT,* 1993 edition. New York: Prentice Hall Travel.

UNIT

25 DIRECT AND INDIRECT SPEECH

1 DIRECT AND INDIRECT SPEECH

Circle the correct words to complete the article about lie detector tests.

The Awful Truth

Recently, the United States Supreme Court said /(told) employers
1.
that you / they were no longer allowed to give lie detector tests (also
2.
called polygraph tests) to people they wanted to hire. Curious about

these tests, I talked to Erica Dale, who took one a couple of years ago.

She was one of the last employees in our organization to take the test.

"The examiner was very nice," she told me. "He asked her / me a
3.
lot of harmless questions at first." During the test, Erica told the

examiner that I / she lived in the suburbs. When he asked, she said
4.
that it was / is Monday and that she took / had taken the bus to
5.   6.
my / her interview. Then he brought up some tougher subjects. "I
7.
told him / you that I got / 'd gotten into trouble for stealing in high
8.   9.
school," Erica said. "There wasn't any point in lying about it."

With its rows of knobs, its wires and coils of paper, a lie detector is

definitely a low-tech piece of equipment. The devices are still used by

police even though experts say that they didn't / don't measure truth,
10.
only physical reactions to questions. Some questions increase a

person's blood pressure and create other physical changes that the

polygraph measures. "The tests <u>are / were</u> only about 50 percent accurate," says one
                                    11.
critic. "They belong in museums."

   Buzz Faye, who served three years for a crime he didn't commit, agrees.

After his arrest, officials gave him a lie detector test. They told him that

<u>we / they</u> <u>plan / planned</u> to drop charges if <u>you / he</u> passed. "Hey, great," said Faye.
   12.   13.   14.
Unfortunately, he failed—twice—and spent three years in jail. Later, someone

<u>said / told</u> the police that Faye <u>didn't commit / hadn't committed</u> the crime. Faye was
   15.   16.
released when the police learned the names of the real criminals.

   A polygraph expert who saw the tests said that police <u>scored / had scored</u> Faye's
                                                                17.
tests improperly. Since his release, Faye has been campaigning against the use of

polygraph tests.

Source: Lisa Davis, "A Doubtful Device," *Health,* October, 1992, pp. 92–95.

② DIRECT AND INDIRECT SPEECH: NECESSARY AND OPTIONAL TENSE CHANGES

*Complete the interviewer's report of this job applicant's statements
during a lie detector test. Change the verb tense for reported speech
only when necessary.*

	The Applicant's Statements During the Test	**The Interviewer's Report Later That Day**
1.	"My name is Anita Bell."	She said her name is Anita Bell.
2.	"It's Wednesday."	_____
3.	"My husband drove me to the interview."	_____
4.	"Our house is near the lake."	_____
5.	"I shoplifted a lipstick once as a teenager."	_____
6.	"I went to my mother right away."	_____
7.	"She took me to the store to return the lipstick."	_____
8.	"I always tell the truth."	_____
9.	"The test seems easy."	_____
10.	"I don't mind taking it."	_____

❸ DIRECT AND INDIRECT SPEECH

Compare another job applicant's statements with his previous employer's information form. Report the statements and then write, **That's true** *or* **That's not true***.*

BATES DEPARTMENT STORE
EMPLOYEE INFORMATION FORM

Name:	Ethan Taylor
Dates employed:	Feb. 1998–Jan. 2000
Position (start):	Sales clerk
Promotions?	No
How many employees did this employee supervise?	None
Salary:	**Start:** $15,500 per year **Finish:** $17,000
Supervisor's comments:	This employee performed well on the job. He was reliable and he showed initiative in serving customers and keeping the department running smoothly.
Reason for leaving:	Laid off when the store reduced its staff
Eligible for rehire:	Yes

---

1. "My name is Ethan Taylor."

   He said his name is Ethan Taylor. That's true.

2. "I worked at Bates Department Store for three years."

   He said he'd worked at Bates Department Store for three years. That's not true.

3. "I was a sales clerk."

   He said he'd been a sales clerk. That's true

4. "Then I received a promotion to supervisor."

   He said he'd received a promotion to supervisor. That's not true

5. "I supervised five other sales clerks."

   He said he'd supervised 5 other sales clerks. That's not true

6. "I was a reliable employee."

   He said he had been a reliable employee. That's true.

7. "I showed initiative."

He said he'd showed initiative. That's true

8. "My employers liked my work."

He said his employers had liked his work. That's true.

9. "Bates didn't fire me."

He said Bates hadn't fired him. That's not true.

10. "I lost my job because of staff reductions."

He said he'd lost his job because of staff reductions. That's true

11. "I earned $18,500 a year."

He said he'd earned $18,500 a year. That's not true

12. "I got a raise of more than $2,000."

He said he'd got a raise of more than $2,000

INDIRECT SPEECH: TENSE CHANGES

① DIRECT AND INDIRECT SPEECH

Read what John Baker said in 1994. Then use indirect speech and write what a friend reported a year later.

1. "I live in Los Angeles."

   He said that he lived in Los Angeles.

2. "I've been living here my whole life."

   _____

3. "I've experienced many earthquakes."

   _____

4. "This quake was the worst."

   _____

5. "I'll start to rebuild my home this week."

   _____

6. "I must make it stronger."

   _____

7. "I may get government aid next month."

   _____

8. "I can't afford earthquake insurance."

   _____

9. "I had looked into it before."

   _____

10. "I should have bought some then."

    _____

2 DIRECT AND INDIRECT SPEECH

In January 1994 there was a terrible earthquake in Los Angeles, California. Read what people said about the quake, and then report their statements.

1. "I was never so afraid in my life." —*Miriam Shakter, human resources manager*

   She said that she'd never been so afraid in her life.

2. "I felt a sensation of falling." —*Diane Stillman, paralegal*

   _____

3. "We were all pretty well prepared for an earthquake, but not the fire."

   —*Al McNeill, Los Angeles resident*

   _____

4. "You can't save everyone." —*Orville Wright, firefighter*

   _____

5. "I haven't seen anything like it." —*Robert DeFeo, Chief of the Fire Department*

   _____

6. "It felt like a giant hand reaching down and shaking me." —*73-year-old man*

   _____

7. "I'm scared that there's going to be another one." —*eight-year-old girl*

   _____

8. "I'm so glad I'm here!" —*Andrea Donnellan, geophysicist*

   _____

9. "I've been through war in my country, but with the quake, I have no idea what to do."

   —*Nicaraguan woman*

   _____

10. "If they say my house can't be saved, I don't know what I'll do or where I'll go."

    —*Jill Banks-Barad, political consultant*

    _____

❸ INDIRECT STATEMENTS: OPTIONAL TENSE CHANGES

Read this interview between Today's World (TW) *and geophysicist Dr. Ito.*

When the Earth Moves

An Interview with Geophysicist Melissa Ito

TW: *Was the Los Angeles quake the worst in California's history?*

ITO: Not at all. The San Francisco quake of 1906 was much worse.

TW: *Earthquakes aren't very common, are they?*

ITO: Actually, there may be as many as a million earthquakes a year.

TW: *A million a year!*

ITO: Yes. Most quakes take place beneath the ocean surface, so we aren't aware of them.

TW: *I guess that's fortunate.*

ITO: It is. Earthquakes are among the most terrible natural disasters that can happen on earth. They've destroyed large cities, started fires, and even caused tidal waves. Take the 1906 San Francisco quake, for example. Flames destroyed large sections of the city.

TW: *What causes earthquakes?*

ITO: It's difficult to explain. Basically, quakes occur as a result of sudden movement in the rocks below the earth's surface. Forces push against the rocks, and the rocks break along lines called *faults.* In fact, it was a hidden fault that caused the January 1994 Los Angeles quake.

TW: *Southern California gets more than its fair share of quakes, doesn't it?*

ITO: Yes. It has had seven strong quakes since 1988.

TW: *Can't scientists predict them?*

ITO: Not really. They can tell you where one will occur but not when.

TW: *That's terrible. Isn't there anything we can do?*

ITO: Yes. There are things we can do. Engineers have developed houses and other structures that are able to withstand earthquake shocks. Governments must enforce building requirements in earthquake zones. That might limit the damage when a quake occurs.

*Read the statements. Write **That's right** or **That's wrong** and report
what the geophysicist said. Remember that you don't always have to
change the tense in indirect speech.*

1. The Los Angeles quake wasn't as bad as the quake that hit San Francisco in 1906.

   That's right. She said that the San Francisco quake of 1906 had been much worse.

2. Earthquakes aren't common.

   That's wrong. She said there may be as many as a million earthquakes a year.

3. Most quakes take place under water.

   right

4. Earthquakes have destroyed large cities and started other disasters.

5. There was a lot of fire damage to San Francisco in 1906.

6. Earthquakes occur as the result of volcanoes.

7. A visible fault caused the 1994 Los Angeles quake.

8. Southern California gets a lot of quakes.

9. Scientists can predict them.

10. There is nothing we can do about quakes.

11. Engineers have developed buildings that can survive earthquakes.

12. Governments are responsible for seeing that building regulations are followed.

INDIRECT INSTRUCTIONS, COMMANDS, REQUESTS, AND INVITATIONS·

❶ DIRECT AND INDIRECT SPEECH

Write sentences in direct and indirect speech. Choose between **She told me** *and* **She asked me** *for the sentences in indirect speech.*

1. (Direct speech)   "Turn left."

(Indirect speech) _She told me to turn left._

2. (Direct speech)   "Don't turn right."

(Indirect speech) _____

3. (Direct speech)   _____

(Indirect speech) She told me to slow down.

4. (Direct speech)   _____

(Indirect speech) She told me not to drive so fast.

5. (Direct speech)   "Can you please turn on the radio?"

(Indirect speech) _____

6. (Direct speech)   _____

(Indirect speech) She asked me to open the window.

❷ AFFIRMATIVE AND NEGATIVE COMMANDS

Read the advice that TV news commentator John Stossel gave viewers about the common and very dangerous problem of feeling sleepy when driving. Rewrite his advice in indirect speech.

John Stossel said:

1. Pull over and take a brief nap.

He told viewers to pull over and take a brief nap.

2. Don't take a long nap.

_____

3. Sing to yourself.

_____

4. Turn the radio to an annoying station.

_____

5. Don't drink coffee.

_____

6. Open the window.

_____

7. Be careful where you take a nap.

_____

8. Don't stop on a deserted roadside.

_____

9. Don't drink and drive.

_____

Source: "20/20," January 21, 1994, ABC-TV.

3 INDIRECT SPEECH

Complete this journal entry by circling the correct words.

Last Friday my neighbor phoned me. She (invited) / told me to go for a ride in her new car.
        a.
I told her I would love to. As soon as I got into the car, she _told / invited_ me to buckle my seat
                                                              b.
belt. I was pleased because I thought this meant she was a safe driver. Was I in for a surprise!

I watched in dismay as the speedometer approached and then passed 70 mph. I told her

slow / to slow down. I begged her _not to / to not_ speed.
   c.   **d.**
    She slowed down for a while, but then she sped up again. Suddenly we heard a siren.

The police officer signaled us to pull over and stop. He got out of the car and asked her

to show / not to show him her license. She only had a learner's permit! He _advised / ordered_
     e.   **f.**

(continued on next page)

her to give him the permit, and, after checking <u>my</u> license, he <u>told / invited</u> me to take the
g.
wheel and follow him to the police station. Two hours later, on the way home from the station,

my neighbor <u>invited / ordered</u> me to have dinner at her place. She had just bought a new
h.
microwave oven that she wanted to try out. I thanked her but told her I had a headache and

needed to take a nap.

4 DIRECT SPEECH

Reread the story in Exercise 3. Rewrite the indirect speech as direct speech.

Would you like to go for a ride in my new car?
a.

b.

c.
d.

e.

f.

g.

h.

INDIRECT QUESTIONS

1 WORD ORDER

Lydia Chan interviewed her grandmother for a family history project at school. The next day, her grandmother told a friend about their talk. Use the words in parentheses and write Lydia's questions as her grandmother reported them.

1. "Can I talk to you about your life?"

   She asked if she could talk to me about my life.
   (about my life / if / could / she / talk to me)

2. "Do you have time today?"

   _____
   (whether / had / I / time / yesterday)

3. "Could you show me some photos?"

   _____
   (could / I / if / show her some photos)

4. "What's your full name?"

   _____
   (was / my full name / what)

5. "Who chose your name?"

   _____
   (who / my name / had chosen)

6. "When were you born?"

   _____
   (born / I / when / was)

7. "What country did your family come from?"

   _____
   (my family / what country / had come from)

8. "Where were you born?"

   _____
   (where / I / born / was)

9. "What was your biggest adventure?"

   _____
   (my biggest adventure / had been / what)

10. "What are you most proud of?"

   _____
   (was / I / what / most proud of)

2 CHANGES IN INDIRECT QUESTIONS

Complete the article by changing the direct questions in parentheses to indirect questions.

BRINGING HISTORY HOME
by Michael Lubecki

A poor young man who had just arrived in the United States saw a fruit

vendor on a New York street. He pointed at a piece of fruit and paid for it. But he

didn't ask _____ what it was _____. He bit into what he thought was an
1. (What is it?)

orange and quickly spit it out. It was a bitter kumquat—and he had spent

precious money on it!

The young man was my grandfather. My mother told the story countless times,

always with the same sad little smile. I loved hearing it and interrupted with

questions to prolong it. I always asked _____.
2. (How old was he?)

"Nineteen," she reported. Then I asked _____. "Five
3. (How much did it cost?)

cents." Finally, I demanded to know _____. She always
4. (Why didn't he ask the name of the fruit?)

replied impatiently, "You know he couldn't speak English."

As an adult, I asked myself _____. Later, I learned that
5. (Why did the details seem so important?)

our story was a typical immigrant family story. Children in a new country

couldn't ask _____, so the family told a story that
6. (How are we going to get by?)

explained the methods they used to survive. (Our family's rule was "Ask

questions!")

Everyone has good stories, and collecting them is an interesting way for younger family members to stay close to older relatives and learn the family's culture. Recently, my son Mark interviewed his grandfather, my husband's father. If you'd like to try this in your family, here are the steps Mark took to make his grandfather feel at ease.

1. Mark asked him politely _____.
   7. (Do you have some time to talk to me?)

2. He found a quiet room to talk in and then asked his grandfather

   _____.
   8. (Do you feel comfortable here?)

3. To get started, Mark talked about an event that the two of them had

   shared. He asked his grandfather _____.
   9. (Do you remember our trip to the circus?)

When the interview got under way, Mark wanted to know about the details of his grandfather's life as a child. He asked him _____
10. (What did you wear to school?)
and _____. He also asked _____.
11. (What did your mother cook?)   **12. (What hobbies did you have?)**
When Mark asked him _____, he learned how his
13. (What was your most important decision?)
hobby, amateur radio, led to his job in communications. When he asked

_____, he learned about his grandfather's fascination
14. (What new invention do you like best?)
with computers.

In this interview, Mark discovered things that we, his parents, had never known about our own parents' generation and ideas.

❸ INDIRECT QUESTIONS

A reporter interviewed Maya Angelou, an American poet who has lived a very interesting life. Read the interviewer's notes and report which of his questions he asked and which ones he didn't ask.

1. when/born?

2. who/gave the nickname Maya?   brother Bailey (called her "Mine")

3. where/grew up?   St. Louis and San Francisco

4. why/moved to San Francisco?

5. what/studied?   dance and drama in a special high
                                          school

6. worked during high school?   yes—streetcar conductor, cook,
                                          singer, dancer

7. ever lived in another country?   yes—in Egypt—with husband, a lawyer from South Africa

8. speak other languages?   yes—fluent in French, Spanish, Italian, Arabic, and Fanti

9. why/name first book
    <u>I Know Why the Caged Bird Sings</u>?

10. why/started writing?   inspired by speech by Dr. Martin Luther King

11. studied writing?

12. where/like to write?   in a motel room near her home

1. ___He didn't ask her when she was born._____

2. ___He asked her who had given her the nickname Maya._____

3. _____

4. _____

5. _____

6. _____

7. _____

8. _____

9. _____

10. _____

11. _____

12. _____

EMBEDDED QUESTIONS

① EMBEDDED QUESTIONS: WORD ORDER AND PUNCTUATION

Complete the conversation by changing the direct questions in parentheses to embedded questions. Remember to punctuate the sentences correctly.

A: Do you know _____ if there's anything good on TV? _____
1. (Is there anything good on TV?)

B: There's World Cup soccer this evening. It's the final match.

A: I don't understand _____
2. (Why do you enjoy watching sports all the time?)

B: Well, I always wonder _____
3. (How can you watch those boring news specials?)

Let's find out _____
4. (What's playing at the movies?)

A: Let's see _____
5. (Can we agree on a movie?)

Do you know _____
6. (Where's today's paper?)

B: I think I saw it in the kitchen.

A: I can never remember _____
7. (What section are the movies in?)

B: They're right behind the sports pages.

A: I don't know _____ It's called
8. (Will you enjoy this one?)

White Lies. It's a romantic comedy.

B: I've heard of it. It's supposed to be very good.

I wonder _____
9. (Can we take the kids?)

A: It doesn't say _____
10. (What's the rating?)

B: Why don't we just get a sitter and go ourselves?

A: That's an excellent idea. Now all we have to do is find out

_____
11. (Is the sitter free tonight?)

2 EMBEDDED QUESTIONS: WORD ORDER AND PUNCTUATION

Choose the appropriate question from the box and change it to an embedded question. Remember to punctuate the sentences correctly.

> Why did they decide to get married?
> How much should we tip the driver?
> Is there parking near the theater?
> Are there any empty seats?
> What time does the movie start?
> ~~Can you baby-sit?~~
> Who is that actor?
> Why doesn't the car start?
> What time is it?
> Where's Merlin Boulevard?
> Do I have enough money?

1. **A:** I wonder ___if you can baby-sit._____

   We want to go to a movie tonight.

   B: Sure. What time do you want me to come over?

2. **A:** Do you know _____

   B: At seven and nine o'clock.

3. **A:** Can you tell me _____

   B: Yes, there is. Parking isn't a problem.

4. **A:** Do you know _____

   B: Merlin Boulevard? Sure. It's easy to get there.

5. **A:** I wonder _____

   B: Try once more. If it doesn't start, we'll call a taxi.

6. **A:** Quick. Can you figure out _____

   B: Let's see. Fifteen percent of eight dollars. Tip her about a dollar and a half.

7. **A:** I think we're late. Do you know _____

   B: It's only 8:40. Relax.

8. **A:** Uh-oh. Ticket prices have gone up. I'm not sure _____

   B: We have enough. I got cash from the ATM today.

9. **A:** It's crowded. I wonder _____

   B: Let's sit toward the back. I think I see two seats.

10. A: I can't remember _____, but I know I've seen him

before.

B: He was the cop in *Mobsters,* wasn't he?

11. A: So, did you like the movie?

B: Yeah, but I'm a little confused. Could you explain _____

They didn't seem to like each other.

A: Because it's a comedy. It has to have a happy ending.

③ INFINITIVES AFTER QUESTION WORDS

Read these conversations from the movie. Write a summary sentence for each one. Use a question word and the infinitive form of the appropriate verbs.

1.   **HE:** I wish I could meet her, but how?

SUMMARY: He can't figure out ___how to meet her._____

2.   **SHE:** What am I going to wear? The black dress? No, too formal.

SUMMARY: She's not sure _____

3.   **HE:** How long do you want to stay at the party?

SHE: Oh, I don't know. Maybe another half hour.

SUMMARY: They're discussing _____

4.   **HE:** I'd like to send some long-stemmed roses.

CLERK: How many?

HE: *[To himself]* Hmm. Is two dozen enough?

SUMMARY: He needs to decide _____

5.   **SHE:** I'm so angry, I think I'll, I'll . . .

FRIEND: Well, what are you going to do?

SHE: I don't know yet, but something!

SUMMARY: She doesn't know _____

6.   **SHE:** When should we get married, June or September?

SUMMARY: She wonders _____

(continued on next page)

7. **FRIEND:** Who's going to be your best man?

    HE: I'm still thinking about it. I'm going to ask either my brother or my college roommate.

SUMMARY: He hasn't decided _____

8. **HE:** Where should we go on our honeymoon?

    SHE: How about Las Vegas?

SUMMARY: She's suggesting _____

 EDITING

Read this letter. Find and correct six mistakes in the use of embedded questions. The first mistake is already corrected.

> *Friday, May 15*
>
> *Dear Alicia,*
>
> *I don't know when ~~are you~~* you are *leaving for your trip, but I decided to write anyway. How are you? Dan and I and the kids are all fine. Busy as usual. Tonight Dan and I got a baby-sitter and went to the movies (we hardly ever have the chance to go out alone). We saw a romantic comedy called <u>White Lies</u>. I don't know is it playing near you, but I recommend it.*
>
> *I was thinking about our last class reunion. Can you remember where it was. I know it was in some restaurant, but I can't remember what the restaurant was called.*
>
> *I've been wondering why I haven't heard from Wu-lan? Do you know where did he move? I'd like to write to him, but I don't know how to contact him.*
>
> *Well, the summer is almost here. Let us know when can you come for a visit. It would be great to see you again.*
>
> *All my best,*
>
> *Lily*

ANSWER KEY

In this answer key, where the contracted form is given, the full form is also correct, and where the full form is given, the contracted form is also correct.

PART I PRESENT AND PAST: REVIEW AND EXPANSION

UNIT 1 SIMPLE PRESENT TENSE AND PRESENT PROGRESSIVE

1

2. ask, asking
3. begin, begins
4. bites, biting
5. buys, buying
6. come, comes
7. digs, digging
8. do, doing
9. employ, employs
10. fly, flies
11. forgets, forgetting
12. have, having
13. lie, lies
14. manages, managing
15. promise, promises
16. say, saying
17. studies, studying
18. travel, travels
19. uses, using
20. write, writing

2

1. b. Are . . . taking
   c. is studying
   d. 's
   e. 'remember
   f. look
2. a. Do . . . know
   b. 's taking
   c. does . . . mean
   d. don't know
3. a. do . . . spell
   b. have
   c. looks

4. a. are . . . doing
   b. seem
   c. 'm trying
   d. is
   e. types
5. a. Do . . . want
   b. does . . . do
   c. analyzes
   d. write
   e. sign
6. a. are . . . doing
   b. 'm writing
   c. 'm reading
   d. think

3

2. doesn't know
3. is thinking
4. is writing
5. looks
6. studies
7. believe
8. tells
9. are using OR use
10. does . . . hope OR is . . . hoping
11. look
12. tells
13. Does . . . lean
14. indicates
15. represents
16. is planning
17. doesn't leave
18. avoids
19. show
20. 're reading
21. is investigating
22. thinks
23. takes
24. warns
25. doesn't guarantee

4

Justin—I hope you ~~don't~~ **aren't** feeling angry at me about my last e-mail. Remember that I wrote, "I ~~not~~ **don't** want to hear from you again! '-)" That little symbol at the end means, "I'm winking, and I ~~only joke~~ **'m only joking**." We ~~using~~ **use OR are using** a lot of these symbols in e-mail. We ~~are calling~~ **call** them emoticons because they show how we are feeling at the moment.

Here are some more:

:-) I ~~smile~~ **'m smiling**.

:-D I'm laughing.

:-(I'm frowning.

8-] Wow! I **'m** really surprised!

(:: ( ) ::) This is ~~meaning~~ **means**, "I want to help." It looks like a Band-Aid.

:-C I ~~'m not believing~~ **don't believe** that!

Please write back soon and tell me that ~~your~~ **you're** not angry. ((((Justin)))) Those are hugs! Delia

UNIT 2 SIMPLE PAST TENSE AND PAST PROGRESSIVE

1

2. apply
3. was OR were
4. became
5. developed
6. eat
7. feel
8. got
9. grew
10. lived
11. meet
12. pay
13. permitted
14. planned
15. said
16. send
17. slept
18. understood

2

2. met
3. asked
4. Was
5. did . . . hate
6. Were . . . going to marry OR Did . . . marry
7. found
8. didn't fall
9. were working
10. met

11. hired
12. was trying
13. was
14. was feeling OR felt
15. was pretending OR pretended
16. thought
17. wanted
18. was working
19. came
20. wasn't going to ask
21. solved
22. stopped
23. fell
24. were taking
25. met
26. became
27. was dating
28. didn't seem
29. heard
30. was whispering
31. had to
32. was going to complain
33. changed
34. wasn't
35. didn't stop
36. broke up
37. asked
38. was moving
39. saw
40. was sitting
41. was parking
42. jumped
43. thought
44. was going to ask
45. was helping
46. looked
47. didn't give up
48. ran into
49. introduced
50. invited

3

I'm really glad that I ~~was deciding~~ **decided** to rent this apartment. I ~~won't~~ **wasn't going to** move here because the rent is a little high, but I'm happy I did. All the others ~~were seeming~~ **seemed** so small, and the neighborhoods just weren't as beautiful as this one. And moving wasn't as bad as I feared. I was planning to take more days off work, but then Hakim ~~offers~~ **offered** to help. What a great brother! We ~~were moving~~ **moved** everything into the apartment in two days. The man next door seemed really nice. On the second

day, he even **helped** ~~help~~ Hakim with some of the heavy

furniture. His name is Jared. I **didn't** ~~don't~~ even unpack

the kitchen stuff last weekend because I was so

tired. Last night I **walked** ~~walking~~ Mitzi for only two

blocks. Jared was standing downstairs and **(was) looking** ~~looked~~

at his mail when I came back. I was going to

ask ~~asked~~ him over for dinner this weekend (in order

to thank him), but everything is still in boxes.

Maybe in a couple of weeks . . .

UNIT PRESENT PERFECT, PRESENT PERFECT PROGRESSIVE, AND SIMPLE PAST TENSE

 1

2. brought, brought
3. chose, chosen
4. delayed, delayed
5. felt, felt
6. found, found
7. finished, finished
8. got, gotten
9. graduated, graduated
10. hid, hidden
11. moved, moved
12. noticed, noticed
13. owned, owned
14. read, read
15. replied, replied
16. ripped, ripped
17. showed, shown
18. spoke, spoken
19. threw, thrown
20. wondered, wondered

2

2. She graduated from college in 1994.
3. She's been reporting OR 's reported crime news since 1997.
4. Recently, she's been researching articles about crime in schools.
5. She's been working on her Master's Degree since 1997.
6. Her father worked for the Broadfield Police Department for twenty years.
7. Simon Pohlig moved to Broadfield in 1992.
8. He's owned Sharney's Restaurant since 1994.
9. He coached basketball for the Boys and Girls Club for two years.
10. He's written two cookbooks for children.
11. He's been planning a local television show for several months.
12. The groom's mother has been serving OR has served as president of TLC Meals, Inc., for two years.

3

2. applied
3. has been working OR has worked
4. found, was
5. has attended
6. began, received
7. went on
8. has been attending OR has attended
9. took
10. didn't get
11. decided
12. hasn't received
13. lived
14. has been living OR has lived
15. looked
16. left, mentioned
17. hasn't told OR didn't tell
18. didn't slant
19. told
20. suggested OR has suggested

4

My son and his girlfriend have **been making** ~~made~~ wedding

plans for the past few months. At first I was

delighted, but last week I **heard** ~~have heard~~ something

that changed my feelings. It seems that our future

daughter-in-law has **decided** ~~been deciding~~ to keep her

own last name after the wedding. Her reasons:

First, she doesn't want to "lose her identity." Her

parents **named** ~~have named~~ her 21 years ago, and she

has been ~~was~~ Donna Esposito since then. She sees no

reason to change now. Second, she is a member

of the Rockland Symphony Orchestra and she

has performed OR has been performing ~~performed~~ with them for eight years. As a result,

she **has already become** ~~already became~~ known professionally by her

maiden name.

John, when I've **got** ~~gotten~~ married, I didn't think

of keeping my maiden name. I **felt** ~~have felt~~ so proud

when I became "Mrs. Smith." We named our son

after my father, but our surname showed that we

three were a family.

I've **read** ~~been reading~~ two articles about this trend,

and I can now understand her decision to use her

maiden name professionally. But I still can't

understand why she wants to use it socially.

My husband and I **have been trying OR have tried** ~~tried~~ to hide our hurt feelings, but it's been getting harder. I want to tell her and my son what I think, but my husband says it's none of our business.

My son ~~didn't say~~ *hasn't said* anything, so we don't know how he feels. Have we ~~been making~~ *made* the right choice by keeping quiet?

~~HASN'T BEEN SAYING~~ *Hasn't said* ONE WORD YET

UNIT 4 PAST PERFECT AND PAST PERFECT PROGRESSIVE

❶

3. entertained
4. cut
5. told
6. withdraw
7. practiced
8. worried
9. seek
10. swept
11. quit
12. led
13. write
14. stolen
15. planned
16. break
17. swum
18. bet
19. sink
20. forgiven

❷

2. had enjoyed
3. had become
4. had started
5. had . . . invented
6. hadn't appreciated
7. had written
8. had been
9. had seen
10. hadn't done
11. had gotten
12. hadn't been
13. had grown
14. hadn't seen
15. had made

❸

2. Had he driven, No, he hadn't.
3. Had he arrived, No, he hadn't.
4. Had he gone, Yes, he had.
5. Had he worked, Yes, he had.
6. Had he met, No, he hadn't.
7. Had he taped, Yes, he had.
8. Had he had OR eaten, No, he hadn't.
9. Had he gone, Yes, he had.

❹

2. Before he appeared in New York City comedy clubs, he had gotten a part-time job as a car mechanic.
3. He wrote for TV after he had moved to Los Angeles.
4. By the time he appeared on "The Tonight Show," he had written for the TV show "Good Times."
5. He had appeared on "The Tonight Show" before he appeared on "Late Night with David Letterman."

6. When he got married, he had already appeared on "Late Night with David Letterman."
7. By the time he did his first prime-time TV show, he had performed at Carnegie Hall.
8. He had had a TV comedy special by the time he did his first prime-time TV show.
9. He had appeared on "The Tonight Show" many times when he became the permanent host of "The Tonight Show."

❺

2. hadn't been doing
3. had been telling
4. had been raining
5. had been eating
6. hadn't been drinking
7. had been crying
8. had been laughing
9. had been washing
10. had been listening
11. had been interviewing
12. hadn't been paying

❻

1. Yes, I had.
2. Had . . . been crying, No, I hadn't.
3. Had . . . been expecting, No, I hadn't.
4. Had . . . been arguing, Yes, we had.
5. Had . . . been traveling, Yes, she had.
6. Had . . . been raining, No, it hadn't.

❼

2. had immigrated
3. had been performing
4. had been working
5. (had been) going
6. had been entertaining
7. had . . . appeared
8. had been counting on
9. had created
10. had not represented
11. had learned

PART II FUTURE: REVIEW AND EXPANSION

UNIT 5 FUTURE AND FUTURE PROGRESSIVE

❶

2. I'll come
3. Are you taking
4. I'll hand
5. It's going to fall
6. You're moving
7. Are you driving, We're flying

8. are you getting, We're going to take
9. I'll drive, we're going to have

❷

2. will be living
3. will be parking
4. won't be preparing
5. will be eating
6. won't be driving
7. will be walking
8. will be moving
9. will . . . be saving

10. won't be buying
11. won't be paying
12. won't be worrying
13. will be providing
14. will be attending
15. will be helping
16. (will be) providing
17. will be seeing

❸

2. will you be using the lawn mower tomorrow? No, I won't.
3. When will we be getting new washers?
4. will you be going to the post office tomorrow? Yes, I will.
5. What will you be making?
6. Who will be watching the kids tomorrow?
7. Will the entertainment committee be planning anything else in the near future? Yes, we will.
8. Will we be meeting every month? Yes, we will.
9. Will we be meeting then? No, we won't.

❹

2. will be meeting with . . . faxes reports
3. attends . . . will be having a phone conference with John Smith
4. has OR eats . . . will be having OR eating lunch with Jack Allen
5. will be billing clients . . . drafts the A & W proposal
6. picks up . . . will be taking Saril to the dentist
7. will be shopping for . . . takes Dursan to the barber
8. pays . . . will be cutting the grass

❺

        'm going
I ~~go~~ to Jack's with the kids in a few minutes. We'll
     playing OR We're going to play   're playing OR we play
be ~~play~~ cards until 10:30 or so. While we'll ~~play~~

cards, Jack's daughter will be watching the kids.
    's going to
It ~~will~~ rain, so I closed all the windows.
                                    starts
Don't forget to watch "ER"! It'll ~~start~~ at 10:00.
'll
I ~~call~~ you after the card game because by the time
                      'll be sleeping
we get home you're ~~sleeping~~.

UNIT 6 FUTURE PERFECT AND FUTURE PERFECT PROGRESSIVE

❶

2. will have completed
3. will have helped
4. will have been using
5. 'll have bought
6. 'll have wrapped
7. won't have planned
8. won't have decided
9. 'll . . . have been arguing
10. won't have wasted
11. 'll have completed
12. 'll have had
13. 'll have participated
14. (will have) redecorated
15. 'll have made
16. 'll have done
17. 'll have straightened
18. 'll have packed
19. 'll have been explaining

❷

1. Yes, I will (have).
2. will . . . have been singing
3. will . . . have sewn
4. will . . . have been waiting
5. will . . . have dried, No, it won't (have).
6. Will . . . have delivered, Yes, they will (have).
7. will . . . have been living OR have lived

❸

2. A: How long will Aida have been walking by August 31?
   B: She'll have been walking (for) a month.
3. A: How many rooms will Arnie have painted by August 5?
   B: He'll have painted three rooms.
4. A: How long will Arnie have been painting downstairs by August 15?
   B: He'll have been painting downstairs (for) four days.
5. A: On August 16, will Arnie have left for his dentist appointment by four o'clock?
   B: Yes, he will (have).
6. A: Will Aida have unpacked all the fall clothing by August 23?
   B: No, she won't (have).
7. A: How long will Aida have been driving in the carpool by August 19?
   B: She'll have been driving in the carpool (for) two weeks.
8. A: How many quarts of blueberries will Corrie have picked by August 19?
   B: She'll have picked three quarts of blueberries.

9. **A:** How many pies will Aida have baked by
August 21?
   B: She'll have baked six pies.
10. **A:** Will they have finished packing for the trip
by August 31?
    B: Yes, they will (have).

PART ||| NEGATIVE QUESTIONS AND TAG QUESTIONS, ADDITIONS AND RESPONSES

UNIT 7 NEGATIVE *YES/NO* QUESTIONS AND TAG QUESTIONS

1

2. doesn't it? No, it doesn't.
3. is it? No, it isn't.
4. haven't you? Yes, I have.
5. does it? Yes, it does.
6. didn't you? Yes, I did.
7. isn't there? Yes, there is.
8. can we? Yes, you can.
9. will you? No, I won't.
10. don't you? Yes, I do.

2

2. Doesn't Greenwood have a public beach? No,
it doesn't.
3. Isn't there an airport in Greenwood? No, there
isn't.
4. Can't you see live theater in Greenwood? No,
you can't.
5. Don't people in Greenwood shop at the mall?
Yes, they do.
6. Isn't the average rent in Greenwood under
$700? Yes, it is.
7. Hasn't Greenwood been a town for more than
a hundred years? Yes, it has.
8. Aren't they going to build a baseball stadium
in Greenwood? Yes, they are.

3

1. **c.** 's
2. **a.** haven't seen
   b. Didn't . . . fill out
   c. shouldn't it
3. **a.** Isn't
   b. Didn't . . . use to be
   c. hadn't been
4. **a.** aren't they
   b. have you
   c. Can't . . . take

4

3. This is a good building, isn't it? OR Isn't this a
good building?
4. The owner takes good care of it, doesn't he?
OR Doesn't the owner take good care of it?
5. He recently redid the lobby, didn't he? OR
Didn't he recently redo the lobby?
6. He doesn't talk very much, does he?
7. The rent won't increase next year, will it?
8. There aren't many vacant apartments, are
there?
9. Some new people will be moving into
apartment 1B, won't they? OR Won't some new
people be moving into apartment 1B?
10. This is really a nice place to live, isn't it? OR
Isn't this really a nice place to live?

UNIT 8 ADDITIONS AND RESPONSES WITH *SO, TOO, NEITHER, NOT EITHER,* AND *BUT*

1

2. has	5. neither	8. do	11. don't
3. did	6. are	9. will	12. so
4. but	7. either	10. too	

2

2. did too
3. neither does
4. so did
5. couldn't either
6. but . . . didn't
7. so is
8. hasn't either
9. So does
10. Neither can
11. So has
12. but . . . don't

3

2. but fish shouldn't
3. and so must dogs OR and dogs must too
4. and neither do fish OR and fish don't either
5. but birds and fish don't
6. but a fish doesn't
7. and so can a fish OR and a fish can too
8. and so will some fish OR and some fish will too
9. but other pets don't
10. and neither do fish OR and fish don't either
11. and so do cats OR and cats do too
12. and neither do birds OR and birds don't either

PART IV GERUNDS AND INFINITIVES

UNIT **GERUNDS AND INFINITIVES: REVIEW AND EXPANSION**

Verb + Gerund: enjoy, forget, stop, practice, recommend, quit, dislike, avoid, love, remember, hate, consider, prefer, give up, feel like

Verb + Infinitive: want, forget, stop, prepare, offer, need, love, remember, hate, decide, learn, promise, prefer, seem, manage

2. watching
3. to recall
4. hearing
5. to calm
6. Sponsoring
7. to limit
8. to participate
9. creating
10. to preview
11. reducing
12. to believe
13. viewing
14. interacting
15. to behave
16. to produce
17. limiting
18. not permitting
19. to watch
20. to understand
21. making
22. to develop
23. (to) get rid of
24. not to make
25. not to continue
26. to avoid OR avoiding
27. not to pay
28. to investigate
29. to offer
30. turning on

3

2. unwilling to change
3. used to putting
4. fed up with seeing
5. likely to hit
6. force . . . to rate
7. hesitate to tell
8. decided to run
9. stopped showing
10. dislike turning off
11. insist on changing
12. forbid turning on
13. permit tuning in
14. dream of owning
15. advise . . . to do
16. keep communicating
17. hesitate to ask
18. agreeing to speak

4

2. A V-chip interferes with their OR them watching violent shows.
3. Beakman encourages them to send in OR their sending in questions.
4. The father objected to Jennifer's OR Jennifer watching cop shows.
5. The teacher recommended their watching "Nick News."
6. Bob didn't remember their OR them seeing that game.
7. Sharif's parents persuaded him not to watch "Z-Men."
8. The mother insisted on Sara's OR Sara turning off the TV.
9. Aziza wanted OR wants Ben to change the channel.
10. Paul can't understand Nick's OR Nick watching the show.

5

I'm tired of ~~hear~~ **hearing** that violence on TV causes violence at home, in school, and on the streets. Almost all young people watch TV, but not all of them are involved in committing crimes! In fact, very few people choose ~~acting~~ **to act** in violent ways. ~~To watch~~ **Watching** TV, therefore, is not the cause.

Groups like the American Medical Society should stop ~~to try~~ **trying** to tell people what to watch. If we want ~~living~~ **to live** in a free society, it is necessary ~~having~~ **to have** freedom of choice. Children need ~~learn~~ **to learn** values from their parents. It should be the parents' responsibility ~~deciding~~ **to decide** what their child can or cannot watch. The government and other interest groups should avoid ~~to interfere~~ **interfering** in these personal decisions. Limiting our freedom of choice is not the answer. If parents teach their children ~~respecting~~ **to respect** life, children can enjoy ~~to watch~~ **watching** TV without any negative effects.

UNIT **MAKE, HAVE, LET, HELP, AND GET**

2. made
3. let
4. made
5. let
6. got
7. helped
8. had
9. made
10. have
11. made
12. let
13. made

2. didn't let them take
3. had them answer
4. made them hand in
5. didn't let them submit
6. had them write
7. let them come
8. had them submit
9. made them sign
10. had them keep
11. didn't make them go
12. help them do OR to do

❸

2. made Mark OR him work it out himself.
3. made Sara OR her try again.
4. had Robert OR him do his homework OR it over.
5. didn't let the students OR them use a calculator.
6. got the students OR them to help clean up the classroom.

❹

Mrs. Olinski made us ~~to stay~~ stay late again after class today. She wants to help us ~~passing~~ pass OR to pass our next test by giving us extra time to review in class. She won't make us use calculators during the test. She says, "Calculators make students ~~to forget~~ forget how to add two plus two!" She's always trying to get us ~~use~~ to use our brains instead. She has us solve lots of homework problems, and she gets us ~~asking~~ to ask lots of questions in class. She's strict, but I think she's a good teacher. She's definitely dedicated. She even ~~let's~~ lets us call her at home. She's certainly gotten me to learn more than I ever did before. Now, if she could only get me to enjoy math, that would really be an accomplishment!

PART V PHRASAL VERBS

UNIT 11 PHRASAL VERBS: REVIEW

❶

2. up	6. down	10. out	14. down
3. over	7. over	11. up	
4. ahead	8. out	12. down	
5. out	9. back	13. up	

❷

2. cut down	7. gets together
3. put together	8. give out
4. burns up	9. go out
5. sets up	10. go back
6. puts on	11. throws away

❸

1. pick them out
2. empty them out, throw it away
3. set them off, keeps them away
4. hanging them up, set it up
5. write them down, gave them up

❹

Wake ~~out~~ up earlier. (No later than 7:30!)

Work out in the gym at least three times a week.

Lose five pounds. (Give ~~over~~ up eating so many desserts.)

Be more conscious of the environment—
—Don't throw ~~down~~ away OR out newspapers. Recycle them.
—Save energy. Turn ~~on~~ off OR out the lights when I leave the apartment.

Straighten up my room.
—Hang ~~out~~ up my clothes when I take ~~off them~~ them off.
—Put my books back where they belong.
—Give ~~^~~ away some of my old books and clothing that I no longer wear ~~away~~.

Don't put off doing my homework assignments. Hand ~~in them~~ them in on time!

Read more.

Use the dictionary more. (Look ~~over~~ up words I don't know.)

When someone calls and leaves a message, call them back right away. Don't put ~~off it~~ it off!

Get to know my neighbors. Ask them ~~^~~ over for coffee ~~over~~.

UNIT 12 PHRASAL VERBS: SEPARABLE AND INSEPARABLE

❶

2. over	8. into
3. out	9. up
4. off	10. over
5. in (on) OR by	11. out OR away
6. out	12. back
7. on	13. out

❷

1. **b.** figure out
   c. carried out
   d. did . . . over
   e. handed out
   f. caught on
   g. calling . . . up
   h. give up
   i. set up

2. **a.** grown up
   b. ended up
   c. put together
   d. turned on
   e. pushed up
   f. found out
   g. come up with
   h. brought out
   i. caught on

❸

2. get along (well) with him
3. run into her
4. straighten it up
5. get through with it
6. pick them OR some out
7. run out of it
8. bring it out
9. picked it up
10. turn it down
11. cover them up
12. used them up
13. put them away
14. turn it on
15. figure it out

❹

PART VI ADJECTIVE CLAUSES

UNIT 13 ADJECTIVE CLAUSES WITH SUBJECT RELATIVE PRONOUNS

❶

2. whose	6. who	10. that	14. who
3. who	7. whose	11. whose	
4. who	8. which	12. who	
5. that	9. who	13. that	

❷

1. **c.** that OR which
   d. occur
   e. who OR that
   f. stay
   g. who OR that
   h. make
2. **a.** that OR which
   b. don't change
   c. that OR which
   d. remain
   e. whose
   f. end
   g. who OR that
3. **a.** that OR which
   b. helps
4. **a.** that OR which
   b. makes
   c. that OR which
   d. holds

5. **a.** that OR which
   b. surrounds
   c. who OR that
   d. know
6. **a.** that OR which
   b. has
7. **a.** who OR that
   b. has
   c. whose
   d. are
   e. who OR that
   f. consider
   g. who OR that
   h. seize

❸

2. She was visiting her aunt, whose apartment was right across from mine. OR She was visiting her aunt whose apartment was right across from mine.
3. I loved Rebecca's smile, which was full of warmth and good humor.
4. We shared a lot of interests that OR which brought us close together.
5. We both enjoyed ballroom dancing, which was very popular then.
6. We also enjoyed playing cards with some of our friends who lived in the neighborhood.
7. Our friend Mike, who was a professional skier, taught us how to ski.
8. We got married in a ski lodge that OR which was in Vermont.
9. Our marriage, which means a lot to us both, has grown through the years.
10. We have two children, who are both in school.
11. We both have jobs that OR which are important to us.
12. I really love Rebecca, who is not only my wife but also my best friend.

UNIT **14** **ADJECTIVE CLAUSES WITH OBJECT RELATIVE PRONOUNS OR *WHEN* AND *WHERE***

❶

1. **b.** who
2. **a.** who
   b. who
   c. whom
3. **a.** who
   b. who
   c. whose
4. **a.** who
   b. where
   c. whom
5. **a.** which
   b. whose
   c. whom
   d. whose
   e. that

6. **a.** that
   b. where
   c. who
7. **a.** whose
   b. whose
   c. who
   d. which
   e. who
   f. whom

❷

2. where
3. thanks
4. whose
5. has found OR found
6. which OR that
7. writes
8. which OR that
9. reads
10. which OR that
11. face
12. when OR that
13. runs out OR has run out
14. when
15. supported
16. which
17. praised
18. which
19. inserted
20. whom
21. feels
22. whom
23. dedicates OR has dedicated
24. where
25. has
26. which OR that
27. 're supposed to

❸

2. *The Clan of the Cave Bear,* which Auel started researching in 1977, tells the story of a clan of prehistoric people.
3. The clan lived during the Ice Age, when glaciers covered large parts of the earth.
4. The story takes place during a period in the Ice Age when the climate was slightly warmer.

5. The people lived near the shores of the Black Sea, where there are a lot of large caves.
6. Bears, which the clan worshiped, lived in some of the caves.
7. The clan made their home in a large cave in which OR where bears had lived. OR which OR that bears had lived in.
8. One aspect of their lives which OR that Auel describes well is their technical skill.
9. She learned some of the arts that OR which prehistoric people had practiced.
10. In her preface, she thanks a man with whom she studied the art of making stone tools. OR she thanks a man who OR whom OR that she studied the art of making stone tools with.
11. She also thanks an Artic survival expert who OR whom OR that she met while she was doing research.
12. He taught her to make a snow cave on Mt. Hood, where she spent one January night.
13. She went through a difficult time when she couldn't write.
14. A fiction writer whose lecture she attended inspired her to finish her book.
15. *The Clan of the Cave Bear,* which Auel published in 1980, was a best-seller for a long time.

❹

Sentence 8: One aspect of their lives Auel describes well is their technical skill.
Sentence 9: She learned some of the arts prehistoric people had practiced.
Sentence 10: In her preface, she thanks a man she studied the art of making stone tools with.
Sentence 11: She also thanks an Arctic survival expert she met while she was doing research.

❺

For my book report, I read *The Clan of the Cave Bear* by Jean M. Auel. This novel, ~~that~~ *which* is about the life of prehistoric people, took years to research. The main character is Ayla. She is found by a wandering clan after an earthquake kills her family. The same earthquake had destroyed the cave in which this clan had lived, and they are searching for another home. The clan leader wants to leave Ayla to die. She is an Other—a human ~~which~~ *whose* language and culture his clan doesn't understand. However, the leader's sister Iza, ~~whose~~ *who OR whom* Ayla soon calls Mother, adopts her.

The story takes place at a time ~~where~~ **when** human beings are still evolving. Ayla is a new kind of human. Her brain, ~~that~~ **which** she can use to predict and make plans, is different from Iza's and other clan members'. Their brains are adapted to memory, not new learning, ~~whom~~ **which** they fear and distrust. At first, Ayla brings luck to the clan. She accidentally wanders into a place where they find a large cave, perfect for their new home. She is educated by Iza, ~~who's~~ **whose** great knowledge everyone respects. The skills that Iza passes on to Ayla include healing and magic, as well as finding food, cooking, and sewing. However, Ayla's powers make it impossible for her to stay with the clan. She learns to hunt, a skill ~~where~~ **which OR that OR (pronoun deleted)** women are forbidden to practice. Her uncle, ~~that~~ **who OR whom** she loves very much, allows her to stay with the clan, but after he dies, she loses his protection. Another earthquake, for which she is blamed, destroys the clan's home, and she is forced to leave.

PART VII MODALS: REVIEW AND EXPANSION

UNIT 15 MODALS AND MODAL-LIKE VERBS: REVIEW

1

2. necessity
3. future possibility
4. assumption
5. assumption
6. necessity
7. prohibition
8. advice
9. future possibility
10. ability

2

2. may not be
3. were able to fulfill
4. could catch
5. 'd better not jump
6. might not sound
7. could harm
8. might shoot
9. doesn't have to use
10. 's able to catch
11. should take care of
12. might not mind

3

2. Should, 'd better not

3. 've got to, can
4. may not
5. must not, ought to
6. has to, should, may
7. 'd better not, weren't able to
8. could, must
9. 'd better, might not
10. can, were we able to
11. 've got to, don't have to
12. can't, should, have got to

4

I have watched all of your shows several times, and I must ~~to be~~ **be** one of your biggest fans. The first time I saw you stick your hand in a nest of poisonous snakes, I ~~might not~~ **couldn't** believe my eyes. In fact, some people have come to the conclusion that you ~~ought to~~ **must OR have (got) to** be crazy to take risks like that. But they still ~~don't able~~ **aren't able to OR can't** to stop watching! Since your show started, you ~~can~~ **have been able to** make a lot of people interested in nature. I am one of those people.

I am a high school senior, and because of your shows, I might major in zoology in college. I'm allowed to take general courses the first two years, so I ~~must not~~ **don't have to** choose my major yet. One of my problems is that I'm afraid I ~~couldn't~~ **won't be able to** find a job when I graduate. What is your opinion? Will there be a lot of jobs in this field in the next few years? My other problem is that my parents don't want me to work with animals. They haven't actually said, "You ~~don't have to~~ **must not OR can't** major in zoology," but they are very worried. What can I ~~to tell~~ **tell** them? I hope you will be able to find the time to answer this letter.

UNIT 16 ADVISABILITY AND OBLIGATION IN THE PAST

1

2. could . . . have done
3. Should . . . have let
4. Yes, you should have
5. could have let
6. might have discussed
7. should . . . have done
8. shouldn't have adjusted
9. ought to have faced
10. tried

11. Should . . . have ignored
12. No, you shouldn't have
13. ought to have told
14. might have acted
15. Should . . . have complained
16. No, you shouldn't have
17. ought to have been able
18. shouldn't have spent
19. shouldn't have called
20. might have tried
21. could have admitted

②

2. They ought to have created a budget with some "personal" money for each partner.
3. He might have treated her attitude with respect.
4. She shouldn't have accused him of irresponsibility.
5. They should have planned ahead.
6. They could have scheduled time alone with each other.
7. He shouldn't have sulked.
8. She ought not to have pretended to be sick.
9. They might have started with small tasks.
10. They could have provided containers to help organize the toys.
11. He shouldn't have given up and done it himself.
12. She shouldn't have expected 100 percent change overnight.

③

I think my new roommate and I have both realized our mistakes. Reggie shouldn't ~~of~~ **have** demanded the biggest room in the apartment as soon as he arrived. He ought **to** have spoken to me first—after all, I've lived here longer than he has. On the other hand, I really shouldn't ~~shout~~ **have shouted** at him as soon as he asked me. I could have ~~control~~ **controlled** my temper and just talked to him about the problem first. I felt really bad about that—until he invited friends over the night before I had to take a test! Then I got so angry, I couldn't sleep. He might ~~of~~ **have** asked me first! I ~~oughta~~ **ought to** have said something right away, but I didn't want to yell again. Of course, some of my habits make Reggie mad too. For example, I could've started washing my

dishes when he moved in, but I just let them pile up in the sink. That was pretty gross—I definitely shouldn't have ~~did~~ **done** that. But then he dumped all the dirty dishes in my bedroom. *He* might **have** found a better way to tell me he was annoyed. Last week, he wanted to talk about our problems. As soon as we started, I realized we should have ~~talk~~ **talked** right away. Things have worked out a lot better since our discussion.

UNIT 17 SPECULATIONS AND CONCLUSIONS ABOUT THE PAST

①

2. couldn't have
3. must have
4. might have
5. must have
6. must have
7. might have
8. may have
9. may have
10. couldn't have
11. had to have

②

2. must not have been
3. had to have felt
4. must have occupied
5. may have traded
6. couldn't have lived
7. may not have been
8. must have fought
9. may have been
10. might not have produced
11. could have gone
12. might not have had
13. may have suffered
14. could have led
15. might have destroyed
16. could have been

③

2. It must have been
3. He might have
4. He might have
5. She could have
6. It must have been
7. They must have
8. He might not have been
9. It couldn't have been

PART VIII THE PASSIVE

UNIT THE PASSIVE: OVERVIEW

1

3. Alice and Jay were fired.
4. The copies were delivered yesterday.
5. Al Baker wrote the article.
6. They frequently hire new editors.
7. The new editor was interviewed by Marla Jacobson.
8. They gave Marla an assignment on the Philippines.

2

2. were called	6. were formed
3. is known	7. were not given
4. is made up	8. is called
5. are considered	9. is OR was named

3

3. are inhabited	8. cover
4. are found	9. contain
5. damage	10. are found
6. cause	11. are used
7. was covered	12. inhabit

4

3. were followed by groups from Indonesia
4. are spoken
5. are understood by speakers of other dialects
6. was declared by President Manuel Quezon
7. was spoken by 55 percent of the Filipinos
8. is spoken by 43 million people
9. is spoken
10. is used

5

2. What other minerals are mined? Gold and silver (are mined).
3. Where are fruits and nuts grown? (They're grown) In the north OR northeast and in the central part of the country.
4. Where is logging done? (It's done) In the east.
5. What animals are raised? Sheep, cattle, and llamas (are raised).
6. Are llamas found in the east? No, they aren't.
7. Are potatoes grown? Yes, they are.
8. Where is rubber produced? (It's produced) In the north.
9. Where is oil found? (It's found) In the south, east, and west OR northwest.

10. Is wheat grown in the north? No, it isn't.
11. Are cattle raised in the east? Yes, they are.

UNIT THE PASSIVE WITH MODALS AND MODAL-LIKE EXPRESSIONS

1

2. Some new airports will be constructed on islands.
3. They might put passenger facilities on decks under the runways.
4. A lot of space could be saved that way.
5. The Japanese had to build an island airport in Osaka Bay.
6. At the old airport, all the air traffic couldn't be handled.
7. They had to move huge amounts of earth from nearby mountains.
8. Travel will be made safer by Hong Kong's new island airport.
9. Travelers can reach the new airport easily.
10. Before, Lantau could be reached by ferry only.

2

2. can be connected
3. will be started
4. may be completed
5. are going to be linked
6. can . . . be carried
7. may not be driven
8. are able to be transported
9. could be joined
10. will be called
11. will . . . be built
12. must be bridged
13. have to be developed
14. will be built
15. will be included
16. might not be fulfilled
17. can't be avoided
18. will be solved

3

2. No, they can't
3. Do . . . have to be occupied
4. No, they don't
5. Must . . . be purchased
6. Yes, they must
7. Is . . . going to be expanded
8. Yes, it is
9. Will . . . be offered
10. Yes, they will
11. Can . . . be purchased
12. Yes, it can

UNIT 20 THE PASSIVE CAUSATIVE

1

2. I'm having OR getting my house painted.
3. I had OR got my car checked last month.
4. We've just had OR gotten our windows cleaned.
5. We must have OR get our repairs done.
6. We're going to have OR get our roof fixed.
7. I'll have OR get my hair cut by Marie.
8. We should have OR get our electric wiring checked.

2

2. have . . . completed
3. have . . . done
4. get . . . tested
5. have . . . replaced
6. have . . . investigated
7. had . . . installed
8. get . . . replaced
9. didn't have . . . done
10. had . . . tested
11. have . . . checked out
12. have . . . stopped
13. have . . . put
14. getting . . . publicized

3

2. How often do you get it done?
3. Did you get it winterized?
4. Have you ever gotten snow tires put on?
5. Are you going to get OR Will you get OR Are you getting snow tires put on for the trip?
6. How often have you gotten it checked since then?
7. Why do you get it done there?

4

3. He didn't have OR get the undercarriage inspected.
4. He had OR got the body and chassis lubricated.
5. He had OR got the air filter inspected.
6. He didn't have OR get the air filter replaced.
7. He didn't have OR get the tires rotated.
8. He didn't have OR get the timing and engine speed adjusted.
9. He had OR got the automatic transmission serviced.
10. He had OR got the cooling system flushed.

5

We've just ~~have~~ **had** our furniture brought over from the apartment, and we're really excited about moving into our "new" (but very old) house. A nineteenth-century millionaire had this place ~~build~~ **built** for his daughter ~~by a builder~~. We were able to afford it because it's a real "fixer-upper." It needs to ~~has~~ **have** a lot of work done. We've already gotten the roof ~~fix~~ **fixed**, but we're not having the outside ~~painting~~ **painted** until fall. After we get **the plumbing repaired** ~~repaired the plumbing~~, we'll paint the inside ourselves (we can't paint over those big water stains!). It sounds awful, but just wait until you see it. There's a fireplace in every bedroom— we're ~~get~~ **getting** OR **going to get** the chimneys cleaned before winter. And the windows are huge. If fact, they're so large that we can't wash them ourselves, so yesterday we had ~~done them~~ **them done** professionally.

As you can imagine, we've both been pretty busy, but we'd love to see you. Are you brave enough to visit us?

PART IX CONDITIONALS

UNIT 21 FACTUAL CONDITIONALS: PRESENT

1

3. That's right.
4. That's wrong. If you travel in September, your ticket costs more than if you travel in October.
5. That's wrong. If you fly in May, you pay off-season rates.
6. That's wrong. If you buy a one-way ticket, you pay more than half the cost of a round-trip ticket.
7. That's right.
8. That's right.
9. That's wrong. If you leave from Washington, you pay the same fare as from Philadelphia.
10. That's wrong. If you fly from Philadelphia, you pay a lower fare than from Chicago.

2

2. If you're flexible, don't go in the summer.
3. If you don't want to spend a lot of money getting around in Rome, take public transportation.
4. If you don't like to book hotels in advance, go to one of the Rome Provincial Tourist Offices.
5. If you prefer small hotels, stay at *pensiones*.
6. If your husband is very interested in architecture, you must visit the Palazzo Ducale in Venice.
7. If you love opera, you should attend an open-air performance in Verona's Roman Arena.
8. If you're interested in seeing ancient ruins, you might want to consider a side trip to Ostia Antica.
9. If you plan to take a hair dryer and an electric shaver with you, don't forget to take a transformer and an adapter.
10. If you want to have a really good dinner your first night there, you should try Sabatini's.

3

3. You should bring along copies of your prescriptions if you take prescription medication.
4. Notify the flight attendant or train conductor if you feel sick on board a plane or train.
5. Call your own doctor if you are traveling in your own country when you feel sick.
6. Your hotel can recommend a doctor if you need medical attention in a foreign country.
7. If you experience chest pains, weakness in an arm or leg, or shortness of breath, get yourself to an emergency room.
8. If you're not sure how serious your symptoms are, assume they are serious and take appropriate steps.
9. Don't drive to the hospital if you need to go to the emergency room.
10. If you wear glasses, take an extra pair with you.

UNIT **FACTUAL CONDITIONALS: FUTURE**

1

2. continues
3. unless
4. depend
5. don't save
6. 's going to save
7. unless
8. change
9. if
10. object
11. 'll
12. practice

2

2. will OR is going to grow
3. 'll OR 's going to happen
4. continue
5. 'll OR 're going to run out
6. change
7. discover
8. will OR is going to be
9. are . . . going to be able to OR will . . . be able to
10. find
11. No, we're not. OR we aren't. OR No, we won't.
12. 'll OR 're going to pollute
13. control
14. find out
15. will . . . help OR is . . . going to help
16. Yes, it will. OR it is.
17. won't OR 're not going to make
18. provide
19. believe
20. 'll OR 're going to replace
21. won't OR 're not going to reduce
22. throw away
23. Will . . . cooperate OR are . . . going to cooperate
24. have to
25. becomes
26. will OR 're going to recycle
27. charge
28. 'll OR 're going to reduce
29. will . . . do OR are . . . going to do
30. begin

3

2. You'll feel good about how our clothes are made if you care about the environment.
3. You won't add to landfill problems if you choose our clothes.
4. If price matters to you, our low prices will please you.
5. If you buy now, we'll contribute part of our profit to YES.
6. If you want to look good, you'll love the styling and colors in our new spring collection.
7. Unless you know the facts, you won't make the right choice.

UNIT UNREAL CONDITIONALS: PRESENT

❶

2. had
3. were
4. offered
5. wouldn't eat
6. 'd be
7. had
8. 'd . . . give
9. didn't need
10. 'd offer
11. weren't
12. didn't need
13. 'd share
14. could offer
15. had
16. would taste
17. would taste
18. put
19. had
20. added
21. would be
22. stirred
23. would be
24. knew
25. ate
26. 'd require

❷

2. We wish the soldiers didn't want our food.
3. We wish we didn't have to hide our food from them.
4. We wish we didn't need all our grain to feed the cows.
5. We wish all our beds weren't full.
6. We wish there were enough room for the soldiers.
7. We wish we knew the king.
8. We wish we had a larger soup pot.
9. We wish we could have stone soup every day.

❸

2. If I had potatoes, I'd make potato soup.
3. If my apartment weren't small, I'd invite people over.
4. If steak weren't expensive, we'd eat it.
5. If my daughter weren't sick, I could go to work.
6. If I didn't have bad eyesight, I'd join the army.
7. If the soup had seasoning in it, it wouldn't taste so bland.
8. If I didn't always hide my money, I'd be able to find it now.
9. If I were rich, I'd take vacations.
10. If I had the recipe, I'd make stone soup.

❹

2. If I were you, I'd read a fairy tale.
3. If I were you, I'd try cabbage soup.
4. If I were you, I wouldn't add salt.
5. If I were you, I wouldn't ask for a raise.
6. If I were you, I wouldn't take her to see *Rambo VI* OR to that movie.
7. If I were you, I'd move.
8. If I were you, I'd eat out.

❺

2. Who would look for us if we got lost?
3. Where would we go if it started to rain?
4. Would you be afraid if we saw a bear?
5. If you heard a loud growl, would you be scared?
6. What would you do if you were in my place?
7. What would we do if we ran out of food?
8. If we didn't have any more food, would we make stone soup?

❻

It's 11:00 P.M. and I'm still awake. I wish I ~~was~~ [were] home. If I ~~would be~~ [were] home, I would be asleep by now! But here I am in the middle of nowhere. My sleeping bag is really uncomfortable. If I were more comfortable, I ~~will~~ [would] be able to sleep. What ~~do~~ [would] my friends think if they could see me now?

I'm cold, tired, and hungry. I wish I ~~have~~ [had] something to eat. But all the food is locked up in the van, and everyone else is sound asleep. If I ~~would have~~ [had] a book, I would read, but I didn't bring any books. Tonight, as we sat around the campfire, someone read a story called "Stone Soup." I'm so hungry that even stone soup sounds good to me. If I ~~know~~ [knew] the recipe, I ~~made~~ [would make] it.

Well, I'm getting tired of holding this flashlight (I wish I ~~would have~~ [had] a regular lamp!), so I think I'll try to fall asleep.

UNIT UNREAL CONDITIONALS: PAST

❶

2. had been
3. had found
4. would have been
5. would . . . have seen
6. owned
7. hadn't earned
8. hadn't paid
9. hadn't given
10. wouldn't have survived
11. had gotten

12. would have paid
13. hadn't met
14. would have been
15. would have disapproved
16. had known
17. hadn't agreed
18. would have taken

2

2. We wish Mary Poppins, the new nursemaid, hadn't demanded two days off a month. We wish she hadn't been so stubborn about it.
3. I wish I had made some money for my pictures today. I wish I could have taken Mary Poppins out for tea.
4. We wish Mary Poppins hadn't taken her day off today. We wish she hadn't gone on a magical journey without us.
5. I wish I hadn't taken the children to visit my Uncle Albert on his birthday. I wish Albert hadn't filled up with laughing gas. I wish he hadn't floated on the ceiling.
6. I wish I hadn't stolen Mary Poppins's magic compass tonight. I wish those giant creatures from the four corners of the world hadn't frightened me.
7. We wish Mary Poppins had wanted to stay forever. We wish she hadn't left with the West Wind last night.

3

2. If he hadn't sold candy to train passengers as a boy, he might not have loved model trains as an adult.
3. He would have joined the army in World War I if he hadn't been too young.
4. If his friend Ub hadn't helped him buy a suit, Disney, who was shy, couldn't have met his fiancée's parents.
5. If Disney had owned the rights to his first cartoon characters, his distributor wouldn't have cheated him.
6. If his art lessons hadn't meant a lot to Disney, he wouldn't have paid for lessons for Disney Studio artists.
7. If a bank hadn't loaned Disney $1.5 million, he couldn't have made *Snow White and the Seven Dwarfs*.
8. If the movie hadn't succeeded, the bank would have taken Disney's studio, the film, and Disney's home.
9. If Disney hadn't died in 1966, he would have seen the opening of the EPCOT Center in Florida.
10. If he hadn't been a genius, he might not have overcome his unhappy childhood.

4

4. would . . . have saved
5. had bought
6. had gone
7. would . . . have gone
8. Would . . . have had to
9. hadn't stayed
10. No, you wouldn't have
11. had called
12. would . . . have told
13. Yes, they would have
14. had planned
15. would . . . have enjoyed
16. Yes, you would have

PART **X** INDIRECT SPEECH AND EMBEDDED QUESTIONS

UNIT **25** DIRECT AND INDIRECT SPEECH

1

2. they
3. me
4. she
5. was
6. had taken
7. her
8. him
9. 'd gotten
10. don't
11. are
12. they
13. planned
14. he
15. told
16. hadn't committed
17. had scored

2

2. She said OR told me (that) it's Wednesday.
3. She said OR told me (that) her husband had driven her to the interview.
4. She said OR told me (that) their house is near the lake.
5. She said OR told me (that) she'd shoplifted a lipstick once as a teenager.
6. She said OR told me (that) she'd gone to her mother right away.
7. She said OR told me (that) she'd taken her to the store to return the lipstick.
8. She said OR told me (that) she always tells the truth.
9. She said OR told me (that) the test seemed easy.
10. She said OR told me (that) she didn't mind taking it.

3

3. He said (that) he'd been a sales clerk. That's true.
4. He said (that) he'd received a promotion to supervisor. That's not true.

5. He said (that) he'd supervised five other sales clerks. That's not true.
6. He said (that) he'd been a reliable employee. That's true.
7. He said (that) he'd shown initiative. That's true.
8. He said (that) his employers had liked his work. That's true.
9. He said (that) Bates hadn't fired him. That's true.
10. He said (that) he'd lost his job because of staff reductions. That's true.
11. He said (that) he'd earned $18,500 a year. That's not true.
12. He said (that) he'd gotten a raise of more than $2,000. That's not true.

UNIT INDIRECT SPEECH: TENSE CHANGES

❶

2. He said (that) he'd been living there his whole life.
3. He said (that) he'd experienced many earthquakes.
4. He said (that) that quake had been the worst.
5. He said (that) he would start to rebuild his home that week.
6. He said (that) he had to make it stronger.
7. He said (that) he might get government aid the following month.
8. He said (that) he couldn't afford earthquake insurance.
9. He said (that) he'd looked into it before.
10. He said (that) he should have bought some then.

❷

2. She said (that) she'd felt a sensation of falling.
3. He said (that) they'd all been pretty well prepared for an earthquake, but not the fire.
4. He said (that) you can't OR couldn't save everyone.
5. He said (that) he hadn't seen anything like it.
6. He said (that) it had felt like a giant hand reaching down and shaking him.
7. She said (that) she was scared that there was going to be another one.
8. She said (that) she was (so) glad she was there.

9. She said (that) she'd been through war in her country, but with the quake, she had no idea what to do.
10. She said (that) if they said her house couldn't be saved, she didn't know what she would do or where she would go.

❸

(Answers may vary slightly.)

3. That's right. She said (that) most quakes take place OR took place beneath the ocean surface.
4. That's right. She said (that) earthquakes have OR had destroyed large cities, (have OR had) started fires, and (have OR had) even caused tidal waves.
5. That's right. She said (that) flames had destroyed large sections of the city.
6. That's wrong. She said (that) quakes occur OR occurred as a result of sudden movement in the rocks below the earth's surface.
7. That's wrong. She said (that) it had been a hidden fault that had caused the January 1994 Los Angeles quake.
8. That's right. She said (that) it has OR had had seven strong quakes since 1988.
9. That's wrong. She said (that) they can OR could tell you where one will OR would occur but not when.
10. That's wrong. She said (that) there are OR were things we can OR could do.
11. That's right. She said (that) engineers have OR had developed houses and other structures that can OR could withstand earthquake shocks.
12. That's right. She said (that) governments must enforce OR have OR had to enforce building requirements in earthquake zones.

UNIT INDIRECT INSTRUCTIONS, COMMANDS, REQUESTS, AND INVITATIONS

❶

2. She told me not to turn right.
3. "Slow down."
4. "Don't drive so fast."
5. She asked me to turn on the radio.
6. "Can OR Could you please open the window? OR Please open the window."

❷

2. He told viewers not to take a long nap.
3. He told viewers to sing to themselves.
4. He told viewers to turn the radio to an annoying station.

5. He told viewers not to drink coffee.
6. He told viewers to open the window.
7. He told viewers to be careful where they took OR take a nap.
8. He told viewers not to stop on a deserted roadside.
9. He told viewers not to drink and drive.

 3

b. told f. ordered
c. to slow g. told
d. not to h. invited
e. to show

4

b. (Please) buckle your seat belt.
c. (Please) slow down.
d. (Please) don't speed.
e. (Please) show me your license. OR Would you (please) show me your license?
f. (Please) give me the permit.
g. (Please) take the wheel (and follow me to the police station).
h. Would you like to have dinner at my place?

UNIT INDIRECT QUESTIONS

1

2. She asked (me) whether I had time yesterday.
3. She asked (me) if I could show her some photos.
4. She asked (me) what my full name was.
5. She asked (me) who had chosen my name.
6. She asked (me) when I was born.
7. She asked (me) what country my family had come from.
8. She asked (me) where I was born.
9. She asked (me) what my biggest adventure had been.
10. She asked (me) what I was most proud of.

2

2. how old he had been
3. how much it had cost
4. why he hadn't asked the name of the fruit
5. why the details had seemed so important
6. how they were going to get by
7. if OR whether he had some time to talk to him
8. if OR whether he felt comfortable there

9. if OR whether he remembered their trip to the circus
10. what he had worn to school
11. what his mother had cooked
12. what hobbies he had had
13. what his most important decision had been
14. what new invention he likes OR liked best

3

3. He asked her where she had grown up.
4. He didn't ask her why she had moved to San Francisco.
5. He asked her what she had studied.
6. He asked her if OR whether she had worked during high school.
7. He asked her if OR whether she had ever lived in another country.
8. He asked her if OR whether she speaks OR spoke other languages.
9. He didn't ask her why she had named her first book *I Know Why the Caged Bird Sings*.
10. He asked her why she had started writing.
11. He didn't ask her if OR whether she had studied writing.
12. He asked her where she likes OR liked to write.

UNIT EMBEDDED QUESTIONS

1

2. why you enjoy watching sports all the time.
3. how you can watch those boring news specials.
4. what's playing at the movies.
5. if OR whether we can agree on a movie.
6. where today's paper is?
7. what section the movies are in.
8. if OR whether you'll enjoy this one.
9. if OR whether we can take the kids.
10. what the rating is.
11. if OR whether the sitter is free tonight.

2

2. what time the movie starts?
3. if OR whether there's parking near the theater?
4. where Merlin Boulevard is?
5. why the car doesn't start.
6. how much we should tip the driver?
7. what time it is?
8. if OR whether I have enough money.
9. if OR whether there are any empty seats.
10. who that actor is
11. why they decided to get married?

3

2. what to wear.
3. how long to stay.
4. how many (flowers OR roses) to send.
5. what to do.
6. when to get married.
7. who to ask.
8. where to go.

4

I don't know when ~~are you~~ **you are** leaving for your trip, but I decided to write anyway. How are you? Dan and I and the kids are all fine. Busy as usual. Tonight Dan and I got a baby-sitter and went to the movies (we hardly ever have the chance to go out alone). We saw a romantic comedy called *White Lies*. I don't know ~~is it~~ **if it's** playing near you, but I recommend it.

I was thinking about our last class reunion. Can you remember where it was**?** I know it was in some restaurant, but I can't remember what the restaurant was called.

I've been wondering why I haven't heard from Wu-lan**.** Do you know where ~~did he move~~ **he moved**? I'd like to write to him, but I don't know how to contact him.

Well, the summer is almost here. Let us know when ~~can you~~ **you can** come for a visit. It would be great to see you again.

TEST: UNITS 1–4

DIRECTIONS: *Circle the letter of the correct answer to complete each sentence.*

EXAMPLE:

Mark _____ a headache last night.　　(A) **B C D**
   (A) had　　　　　　　　　　(C) has had
   (B) has　　　　　　　　　　(D) was having

1. Her name is Victoria, but her friends _____ *call* _____ her Vicki.　　**A B C D**
   (A) are calling　　　　　　(C) had called
   (B) call　　　　　　　　　(D) were calling

2. Water ___ *freezes* ___ at 0 degrees C.　　**A B C D**
   (A) freezes　　　　　　　(C) has been freezing
   (B) froze　　　　　　　　(D) is freezing

3. In her latest book, the author ___ *describes* ___ her childhood.　　**A B C D**
   (A) describes　　　　　　(C) has been describing
   (B) is describing　　　　(D) was describing

4. John _____. It really annoys me.　　**A B C D**
   (A) always complain　　　(C) is always complaining
   (B) had always complained　(D) was always complaining

5. I _____ Jackie, but I didn't.　　**A B C D**
   (A) told　　　　　　　　(C) was going to tell
   (B) 've told　　　　　　(D) was telling

6. By 11:00 this morning, I ___ *had drunk* ___ three cups of coffee.　　**A B C D**
   (A) drink　　　　　　　(C) had drunk
   (B) had been drinking　　(D) have drunk

7. I was listening to the radio when I ___ *heard* ___ the news.　　**A B C D**
   (A) hear　　　　　　　(C) 've heard
   (B) heard　　　　　　　(D) was hearing

8. They ___were living___ in Paris when they met for the first time.　　**A　B　C　D**
   (A) lived　　　　　　　　　　(C) 've been living
   (B) 've lived　　　　　　　　 (D) were living

9. Sara always ___wears___ glasses. She can't see without them.　　**A　B　C　D**
   (A) had worn　　　　　　　　(C) is wearing
   (B) has been wearing　　　　 (D) wears

10. Can you please turn down the radio? The baby ___is sleeping___.　　**A　B　C　D**
    (A) has slept　　　　　　　　(C) sleeps
    (B) is sleeping　　　　　　　 (D) slept

11. The Morrisons ___moved___ to Texas last September.　　**A　B　C　D**
    (A) had moved　　　　　　　 (C) have moved
    (B) have been moving　　　　(D) moved

12. While Jedd was living in Toronto, Helen ___was living___ in California.　　**A　B　C　D**
    (A) has lived　　　　　　　　(C) lives
    (B) had lived　　　　　　　　(D) was living

Part Two

DIRECTIONS: _Each sentence has four underlined words or phrases._
The four underlined parts of the sentence are marked A, B, C, and D.
Circle the letter of the <u>one</u> underlined word or phrase that is NOT
CORRECT.

Example:

Rosa <u>rarely</u> <u>is using</u> public transportation, but <u>this morning</u> she　　**A　(B)　C　D**
　　　 A　　 B　　　　　　　　　　　　　　　 C
<u>is taking</u> the bus.
　 D

13. The doctor <u>called</u> <u>this morning</u> <u>while</u> you <u>slept</u>. _were sleeping_　　**A　B　C　D**
　　　　　　　　 A　　　　 B　　　　　 C　　　 D

14. <u>When</u> she <u>was</u> little, they <u>were naming</u> her "Strawberry" because _named_　　**A　B　C　D**
　　　 A　　　　 B　　　　　 C
    she <u>had</u> beautiful red hair.
　　　　 D

15. They <u>were going to</u> <u>drive</u> to the beach, but they <u>have changed</u> their　　**A　B　C　D**
　　　　　　 A　　　　　 B　　　　　　　　　　　 C
    plans when it <u>started</u> to rain.
　　　　　　　　 D

16. <u>By the time</u> I <u>had gotten</u> home, the show <u>had</u> <u>already ended</u>. _got_　　**A　B　C　D**
　　　 A　　　　　 B　　　　　　　　　　 C　　 D

17. Pete and Andy <u>were</u> <u>driving</u> to work <u>when</u> they <u>were seeing</u> the   **A B C D**
                   A   B   C   D
    saw
    accident.

18. Erika <u>has</u> <u>been looking</u> for a job <u>since</u> she <u>has graduated</u> from college.   **A B C D**
            A   B   C   D

19. Janice <u>didn't own</u> a car then because she <u>hasn't</u> <u>learned</u> to drive <u>yet</u>.   **A B C D**
       doesn't
             A   B   C   D

20. I <u>had</u> <u>been living</u> in this apartment for ten years, but <u>I'm</u> <u>looking</u> for   **A B C D**
     have
      A   B   C   D
    a new one now.

Being non-action verb copy

TEST: UNITS 5-6

DIRECTIONS: Circle the letter of the correct answer to complete each sentence.

EXAMPLE:

Mark _____ a headache last night.   (A) B   C   D
   (A) had   (C) has had
   (B) has   (D) was having

1. Bill will be ___*flying*___ to Taipei tomorrow.   A   B   C   D
   (A) flies   (C) fly
   (B) flying   (D) have been flying

2. We ___*will own*___ a new TV soon.   A   B   C   D
   (A) had owned   (C) 're owning
   (B) 'll own   (D) 've owned

3. Look at those dark clouds! It ___*'s going to rain*___   A   B   C   D
   (A) rains   (C) 's raining
   (B) 's going to rain   (D) will rain

4. They'll be making photocopies while he
___*finishes*___ typing the report.   A   B   C   D
   (A) finishes   (C) 'll finish
   (B) 'll be finishing   (D) 's been finishing

5. I ___*won't*___ be working tomorrow. I'll be
out of town.   A   B   C   D
   (A) don't   (C) 'm not
   (B) haven't   (D) won't

6. Kareem will _____ almost $1,000 by
next year.   A   B   C   D
   (A) had saved   (C) have saved
   (B) have been saving   (D) saves

7. We're late. When we ___*get*___ there, they'll
already have eaten dinner.   A   B   C   D
   (A) get   (C) 'll get
   (B) got   (D) 'll have gotten

8. By the end of this week, Henry _____ regularly for   **A B C D**
   six months.
   (A) exercised   (C) will exercise
   (B) exercises   (D) will have been exercising

9. When I finish this mystery story by Nguyen Treng, I'll   **A B C D**
   _____ all of her mysteries.
   (A) be reading   (C) have read
   (B) have been reading   (D) read

10. Next year, the Carters will have been living in that house   **A B C D**
    _____ forty years.
    (A) already   (C) since
    (B) for   (D) yet

PART TWO

DIRECTIONS: *Each sentence has four underlined words or phrases.*
The four underlined parts of the sentence are marked A, B, C, and D.
Circle the letter of the <u>one</u> underlined word or phrase that is NOT
CORRECT.

EXAMPLE:

Rosa <u>rarely</u> <u>is using</u> public transportation, but <u>this morning</u> she   **A Ⓑ C D**
     A   B   C

<u>is taking</u> the bus.
  D

11. <u>Will</u> you <u>been</u> going to the drugstore <u>tonight</u>?   **A B C D**
   A   B   D
(be written above "been")

12. <u>While</u> Bill <u>will wash</u> the dishes, <u>I'll</u> be <u>straightening</u> the living room.   **A B C D**
   A   B   C   D
(is washing written above "will wash")

13. <u>After</u> I <u>finished</u> this lap, <u>I'll have</u> <u>walked</u> three miles.   **A B C D**
   A   B   C   D
(finish written above "finished")

14. Professor Sanek <u>is</u> <u>arriving</u> at 8:00, and he <u>calls</u> you <u>then</u>.   **A B C D**
                  A   B   C   D
(will call written above "calls")

15. The Tokagarus <u>will save</u> <u>for</u> ten years <u>by the time</u> their first   **A B C D**
               A   B   C

   child <u>enters</u> college.
            D

16. Seana will <u>has</u> <u>been</u> watching television <u>for</u> an hour by the time   **A B C D**
           A   B   C

   dinner <u>is</u> ready.
         D

17. In the twenty-first century, most <u>people</u> in this country <u>will</u> <u>be</u> <u>work</u>ing   **A B C D**
                                     A   B C D

   in service jobs.

18. At the end of this year, Tania <u>will</u> <u>have</u> been <u>paying</u> her credit card   **A**   **B**   **C**   **D**

                     A   B   C

bill <u>since</u> three years.

     D

19. She'<u>ll</u> <u>have</u> <u>been paying</u> a total of $3,000 by the time she <u>pays off</u>   **A**   **B**   **C**   **D**

      A   B   C   D

her loan.

20. John loves that old suitcase. By the time he <u>gets</u> home from vacation   **A**   **B**   **C**   **D**

                                carried   A

<u>next month</u>, he'll <u>have</u> <u>carries</u> it at least 50,000 miles.

    B   C   D

TEST: UNITS 7–8

DIRECTIONS: Circle the letter of the correct answer to complete each sentence.

EXAMPLE:

Mark _____ a headache last night. (A) B C D
   (A) had   (C) has had
   (B) has   (D) was having

1. _____ you from Panama?   A B C D
   (A) Aren't   (C) Did
   (B) Come   (D) Didn't

2. Ben's not at work today, _____?   A B C D
   (A) does he   (C) is he
   (B) doesn't he   (D) isn't he

3. Your cousin lived in New York, _____?   A B C D
   (A) didn't she   (C) isn't she
   (B) hadn't she   (D) wasn't she

4. Miguel _____ here very long, has he?   A B C D
   (A) has been   (C) was
   (B) hasn't been   (D) wasn't

5. **A:** Doesn't Sam own a house in Florida?   A B C D
   B: _____ He bought one there last year.
   (A) No, he doesn't.   (C) Yes, he does.
   (B) No, he didn't.   (D) Yes, he did.

6. **A:** Can't Rick speak Spanish?   A B C D
   B: _____ He never learned.
   (A) No, he can't.   (C) Yes, he can.
   (B) No, he doesn't.   (D) Yes, he does.

7. That's your notebook, isn't _____?   A B C D
   (A) there   (C) yours
   (B) it   (D) that

8. A: You're not Alex, are you?   A B C D
   B: _____ I'm Alex Winslow.
   (A) No, I'm not.   (C) Yes, I am.
   (B) No, you're not.   (D) Yes, you are.

9. A: Today's July 5th, isn't it?   A B C D
   B: _____ It's the 6th.
   (A) Neither is it.   (C) So is it.
   (B) No, it isn't.   (D) Yes, it is.

10. They've read the paper, _____ I have too.   A B C D
   (A) and   (C) either
   (B) but   (D) neither

11. A: Jennifer ate at home last night.   A B C D
   B: _____ I saw him having dinner in the school cafeteria.
   (A) But Mike did.   (C) Neither did Mike.
   (B) But Mike didn't.   (D) So did Mike.

12. A: Andrea speaks fluent French.   A B C D
   B: _____
   (A) Neither does Paul.   (C) So is Paul.
   (B) So does Paul.   (D) So Paul does.

13. A: The Mets played well last night.   A B C D
   B: So _____ the Phillies. It was an exciting game.
   (A) did   (C) played
   (B) didn't   (D) were

14. The hotel _____ expensive, and so were the restaurants.   A B C D
   (A) was   (C) were
   (B) wasn't   (D) weren't

PART TWO

DIRECTIONS: Each sentence has four underlined words or phrases.
The four underlined parts of the sentence are marked A, B, C, and D.
Circle the letter of the <u>one</u> underlined word or phrase that is NOT
CORRECT.

EXAMPLE:

Rosa <u>rarely</u> <u>is using</u> public transportation, but <u>this morning</u> she   A (B) C D
    A   B   C
<u>is taking</u> the bus.
  D

15. <u>This</u> <u>isn't</u> the way to Route 101, <u>is</u> <u>this</u>?   A B C D
    A   B   C D

16. Mary <u>works</u> on Saturdays, <u>doesn't</u> <u>Mary</u>?   A B C D
      A   B C   D

17. Jeff <u>bought</u> a new car, <u>and</u> <u>so</u> <u>does</u> Ann.
        A   B C D

                                                       A B C D

18. Rachel <u>didn't</u> <u>go</u> to class today, <u>and</u> her sister <u>did</u>.
           A   B   C   D   **A B C D**

19. I <u>didn't enjoy</u> the movie, <u>and</u> Frank <u>did</u> <u>either</u>.
           A   B   C   D   **A B C D**

20. Vilma <u>is coming</u> to the party, <u>and</u> <u>so</u> <u>Craig is</u>.
             A   B C   D   **A B C D**

TEST: UNITS 9–10

DIRECTIONS: Circle the letter of the correct answer to complete each sentence.

EXAMPLE:

Mark _____ a headache last night.   (A) B   C   D
   (A) had   (C) has had
   (B) has   (D) was having

1. __Making_____ the streets safe again is the   A   B   C   D
   mayor's highest priority.
   (A) Is making   (C) Makes
   (B) Make   (D) Making

2. Geraldo is looking forward to __becoming_____   A   B   C   D
   a father.
   (A) became   (C) becomes
   (B) becoming   (D) become

3. It was very difficult __to find_____ a good job.   A   B   C   D
   (A) find   (C) has found
   (B) found   (D) to find

4. Elliot bought an exercise video __to help_____   A   B   C   D
   him get into shape.
   (A) helped   (C) is helping
   (B) helps   (D) to help

5. It's time __to decide_____ where we want to go   A   B   C   D
   this summer.
   (A) to decide   (C) deciding
   (B) decides   (D) decide

6. I'm sorry, but I forgot __to bring_____ that book   A   B   C   D
   you asked for.
   (A) bring   (C) to bring
   (B) bringing   (D) brought

7. I can't imagine __your doing__ that.   A   B   C   D
   (A) do   (C) you to do
   (B) to do   (D) your doing

8. Pat invited _me to spend_ the weekend with them.   A B C D
   (A) I spend   (C) me to spend
   (B) me spend   (D) my spending

9. The judge made the witness _answer_ the question.   A B C D
   (A) answer   (C) answering
   (B) answered   (D) to answer

10. It's a good idea _to make_ a reservation.   A B C D
   (A) make   (C) made
   (B) makes   (D) to make

11. The defendant denied _owning_ a weapon.   A B C D
   (A) owned   (C) owns
   (B) owning   (D) to own

12. Gary didn't write down the test date, so he didn't   A B C D
   remember _to study_.
   (A) studied   (C) studying
   (B) studies   (D) to study

PART TWO

DIRECTIONS: Each sentence has four underlined words or phrases. The four underlined parts of the sentence are marked A, B, C, and D. Circle the letter of the one underlined word or phrase that is NOT CORRECT.

EXAMPLE:

Rosa <u>rarely</u> <u>is using</u> public transportation, but <u>this morning</u> she   A (B) C D
     A   B   C

<u>is taking</u> the bus.
   D

13. I <u>got</u> all my friends <u>help</u> <u>me</u> <u>move</u> last June.   A B C D
     A   B C D

14. Phil decided <u>changing</u> jobs because his boss always <u>made</u> <u>him</u>   A B C D
               A   B C
   <u>work</u> overtime.
   D

15. The students of Maitlin High <u>appreciated</u> their <u>principal's</u> <u>try</u>   A B C D
                               A   B C
   <u>to improve</u> conditions in their school.
   D

16. Sally is really tired <u>for</u> <u>being</u> responsible for <u>everyone's</u> <u>doing</u> the   A B C D
                  A B   C   D
   work on time.

17. Robert <u>succeeded in</u> <u>to find</u> a job after high school, so his parents   A B C D
               A   B
   <u>didn't make</u> him <u>apply</u> to college.
   C   D

18. If you insist <u>on</u> <u>looking</u> over the report, please <u>don't forget</u> <u>returning</u>   **A B C D**
             A   B   C   D
it by Monday.

19. <u>Going</u> on a diet doesn't <u>seem</u> <u>to be</u> the best way <u>losing</u> weight.   **A B C D**
       A   B   C   D

20. If you're <u>planning</u> <u>to be</u> near the post office today, <u>could</u> you stop   **A B C D**
                A   B   C
<u>buying</u> some stamps?
   D

TEST: UNITS 11–12

PART ONE

DIRECTIONS: Circle the letter of the correct answer to complete each sentence.

EXAMPLE:

Mark _____ a headache last night.   (A) B C D
  (A) had   (C) has had
  (B) has   (D) was having

1. Jan was depressed when the company she wanted   A B C D
   to work for turned _____ her application
   for the job.
   (A) down   (C) on
   (B) off   (D) out

2. Your mother called. She wants you to call   A B C D
   her _____ tonight.
   (A) back   (C) off
   (B) in   (D) over

3. That's very original. How did you dream   A B C D
   _____ that idea?
   (A) about   (C) of
   (B) down   (D) up

4. **A:** It's cold outside. You need your jacket.   A B C D
   B: OK. I'll put _____.
   (A) it on   (C) on it
   (B) it over   (D) over it

5. Some damage was brought _____ by   A B C D
   high winds.
   (A) about   (C) down
   (B) across   (D) through

6. Come in. Please sit _____.   A B C D
   (A) down   (C) it down
   (B) down it   (D) up

7. Every spring, Marta _____ away some clothes to a local charity.   **A B C D**
   - (A) gives
   - (B) keeps
   - (C) puts
   - (D) throws

8. I can hardly hear the TV. Could you turn it _____?   **A B C D**
   - (A) in
   - (B) off
   - (C) on
   - (D) up

9. She ran _____ on the way to the supermarket.   **A B C D**
   - (A) him into
   - (B) into
   - (C) into Jason
   - (D) Jason into

10. It's too cold to take your mittens off. _____   **A B C D**
    - (A) Don't keep them on.
    - (B) Keep on.
    - (C) Keep them.
    - (D) Keep them on.

11. Erika wants to quit, but she says she'll _____.   **A B C D**
    - (A) give up
    - (B) see the project through
    - (C) see through the project
    - (D) see through it

PART TWO

DIRECTIONS: *Each sentence has four underlined words or phrases. The four underlined parts of the sentence are marked A, B, C, and D. Circle the letter of the* <u>one</u> *underlined word or phrase that is NOT CORRECT.*

EXAMPLE:

Rosa <u>rarely</u> <u>is using</u> public transportation, but <u>this morning</u> she   **A (B) C D**
     A   B   C
<u>is taking</u> the bus.
   D

12. Could we talk <u>over it</u> before you <u>turn</u> the whole <u>idea</u> <u>down</u>?   **A B C D**
                     A   B   C D

13. I know I <u>let</u> <u>Andy</u> <u>down</u> when I forgot to pick his suit <u>out</u> from the   **A B C D**
             A   B   C   D
dry cleaner's.

14. I <u>ran into</u> <u>him</u> when I was <u>getting</u> <u>the bus off</u>.   **A B C D**
     A   B   C   D

15. As soon as I <u>hand</u> <u>in</u> <u>my report</u>, I'm going to take all these books   **A B C D**
              A B   C
<u>on</u> to the library.
  D

16. When you <u>come across</u> a new word, it's a good idea to <u>look it</u>   **A B C D**
               A   B   C
<u>in a dictionary up</u>.
      D

17. <u>We'd better</u> <u>get the bus on</u> now, or <u>we</u>'re going to <u>miss it</u>.   **A   B   C   D**
　　　　A　　　　　　B　　　　　　　　C　　　　　　D

18. Instead of <u>calling off</u> the meeting, maybe we can just <u>put it</u> <u>over</u>   **A   B   C   D**
　　　　　　　A　　　B　　　　　　　　　　　　　　C　　D

until next week.

19. If you don't use <u>out</u> the milk by Monday, please <u>throw</u> <u>it</u> <u>away</u>.   **A   B   C   D**
　　　　　　　　　　A　　　　　　　　　　　　　B　　C　　D

20. Greg <u>had to</u> <u>cheer up her</u> after the company <u>turned down</u>   **A   B   C   D**
　　　　　　A　　　　B　　　　　　　　　　　　　C

<u>her application</u>.
　　　D

TEST: UNITS 13–14

PART ONE

DIRECTIONS: *Circle the letter of the correct answer to complete each sentence. Note that a deleted relative pronoun or a deleted* **when (——)** *is a possible correct answer.*

EXAMPLE:

Mark _____ a headache last night.   (A) B C D
- (A) had
- (B) has
- (C) has had
- (D) was having

1. Our house, _____ my grandfather built, was on a busy corner.   A B C D
   - (A) where
   - (B) which
   - (C) whose
   - (D) that

2. Lisa, _____ I've already mentioned, wrote me a letter.   A B C D
   - (A) which
   - (B) whom
   - (C) that
   - (D) ——

3. Those are the people _____ I told you about.   A B C D
   - (A) where
   - (B) which
   - (C) whose
   - (D) ——

4. Do you remember the day _____ we found that old bookstore?   A B C D
   - (A) where
   - (B) which
   - (C) whom
   - (D) that

5. Can you hand me the book _____ is on the top shelf?   A B C D
   - (A) that
   - (B) where
   - (C) who
   - (D) whose

6. Do you know the man _____ sister works in the library?   A B C D
   - (A) that
   - (B) which
   - (C) who
   - (D) whose

7. Mr. Bartolotta, _____ owns the hardware store, comes   **A   B   C   D**
from my father's hometown.
(A) that   (C) whom
(B) who   (D) whose

8. Tell me about the city _____ you grew up.   **A   B   C   D**
(A) that   (C) which
(B) where   (D) ——

9. Tony loved the book _____ I lent him.   **A   B   C   D**
(A) when   (C) whose
(B) who   (D) ——

10. Do you remember Angela, _____ you met at the class party?   **A   B   C   D**
(A) that   (C) who
(B) which   (D) ——

11. The candidate for _____ I voted lost the election.   **A   B   C   D**
(A) that   (C) who
(B) which   (D) whom

12. I often think back on the time _____ we traveled together.   **A   B   C   D**
(A) where   (C) who
(B) which   (D) ——

Part Two

DIRECTIONS: Each sentence has four underlined words or phrases.
The four underlined parts of the sentence are marked A, B, C, and D.
Circle the letter of the <u>one</u> underlined word or phrase that is NOT
CORRECT.

Example:

Rosa <u>rarely</u> <u>is using</u> public transportation, but <u>this morning</u> she   **A (B) C D**
      A   B   C
<u>is taking</u> the bus.
   D

13. The woman <u>who</u> <u>she</u> <u>moved</u> next door <u>is</u> very nice.   **A   B   C   D**
               A   B   C   D

14. One <u>singer</u> <u>who's</u> voice <u>I</u> like <u>is</u> Mary Grant.   **A   B   C   D**
        A   B   C   D

15. The <u>stories</u> <u>what</u> <u>I've told</u> you <u>are</u> all true.   **A   B   C   D**
         A   B   C   D

16. I <u>enjoyed</u> reading the article <u>that</u> you <u>told</u> me about <u>it</u>.   **A   B   C   D**
       A   B   C   D

17. I've read some <u>books</u> <u>that</u> <u>discusses</u> the time <u>when</u> this area was   **A   B   C   D**
                   A   B   C   D
undeveloped.

18. <u>San Francisco,</u> <u>that</u> <u>is</u> a beautiful <u>city,</u> has a population of 6 million.   **A**   **B**   **C**   **D**
        A   B   C   D

19. Do you know <u>whom</u> wrote the <u>song</u> <u>that</u> Al <u>was</u> singing last night?   **A**   **B**   **C**   **D**
                 A   B   C   D

20. That's the man <u>whose</u> sisters <u>works</u> in the store <u>that</u> <u>is</u> on Fifth Street.   **A**   **B**   **C**   **D**
            A   B   C   D

TEST: UNITS 15–17

PART ONE

DIRECTIONS: *Circle the letter of the correct answer to complete each sentence.*

EXAMPLE:

Mark _____ a headache last night.   (Ⓐ) **B**   **C**   **D**
- (A) had
- (B) has
- (C) has had
- (D) was having

1. We're going to be late. We _____ left   **A**   **B**   **C**   **D**
   earlier.
   - (A) should
   - (B) should have
   - (C) shouldn't
   - (D) shouldn't have

2. You _____ Elena. It was a secret.   **A**   **B**   **C**   **D**
   - (A) might have told
   - (B) should have told
   - (C) shouldn't have told
   - (D) should tell

3. **A:** Was it cold last night?   **A**   **B**   **C**   **D**
   B: It _____. The puddles froze.
   - (A) could have
   - (B) had to have
   - (C) had to have been
   - (D) ought to have been

4. You _____ take an umbrella. It isn't   **A**   **B**   **C**   **D**
   going to rain.
   - (A) don't have to
   - (B) have to
   - (C) must
   - (D) must not

5. **A:** Are the Martins at home?   **A**   **B**   **C**   **D**
   B: They _____. None of the lights
   are on.
   - (A) could
   - (B) could be
   - (C) couldn't
   - (D) couldn't be

6. Jack is really unhappy at work. He ought   **A**   **B**   **C**   **D**
   _____ for another job soon.
   - (A) have looked
   - (B) have to look
   - (C) to have looked
   - (D) to look

7. **A:** I'm sorry I'm late.   A   B   C   D
   B: You _____. I've been waiting for an hour.
   (A) might call   (C) might not call
   (B) might have called   (D) might not have called

8. **A:** Should he have called the police?   A   B   C   D
   B: Yes, he _____.
   (A) did   (C) should
   (B) has   (D) should have

9. **A:** Did we pay the electric bill last month?   A   B   C   D
   B: We _____. We got a second notice today.
   (A) could have   (C) must not have
   (B) shouldn't have   (D) should have

10. **A:** I'm sorry I had to cancel our date.   A   B   C   D
    B: Oh, I couldn't have _____ anyway. I got sick.
    (A) been gone   (C) gone
    (B) go   (D) went

11. I'm not paying this bill. They _____ charged us since they   A   B   C   D
    never finished the job.
    (A) might not have   (C) should have
    (B) must not have   (D) shouldn't have

12. **A:** Did they see the Pyramids?   A   B   C   D
    B: They _____. Everyone who visits Egypt sees the
        Pyramids.
    (A) could have   (C) might have
    (B) couldn't have   (D) must have

13. **A:** Could John have been at home?   A   B   C   D
    B: He _____. I don't really know.
    (A) could have   (C) was
    (B) could have been   (D) maybe

14. That's impossible! Janet _____ have known about the party.   A   B   C   D
    (A) couldn't   (C) ought not to
    (B) might not   (D) shouldn't

PART TWO

DIRECTIONS: Each sentence has four underlined words or phrases. The four underlined parts of the sentence are marked A, B, C, and D. Circle the letter of the <u>one</u> underlined word or phrase that is NOT CORRECT.

EXAMPLE:

Rosa <u>rarely</u> <u>is using</u> public transportation, but <u>this morning</u> she   **A Ⓑ C D**
        A   B   C

<u>is taking</u> the bus.
    D

15. I'm not <u>sure</u>, but Mary <u>could</u> <u>of</u> <u>found</u> out about the surprise party.   **A B C D**
             A   B   C   D

16. Fastfoods Restaurant <u>must</u> <u>has</u> <u>gone</u> out of business <u>recently</u>.   **A B C D**
                       A   B   C   D

17. Carlos <u>had to</u> <u>had</u> <u>studied</u> English before he <u>came</u> here.   **A B C D**
         A   B   C   D

18. Felicia <u>didn't</u> <u>wave</u> to me, so she <u>must have</u> <u>seen</u> me.   **A B C D**
         A   B   C   D

19. We <u>ought to have</u> <u>looked at</u> more apartments <u>before</u> we <u>rent</u> this one.   **A B C D**
          A   B   C   D

20. I'm afraid the store <u>may</u> <u>closes</u> before I <u>can</u> <u>get</u> there.   **A B C D**
                    A   B   C   D

TEST: UNITS 18–20

PART ONE

DIRECTIONS: Circle the letter of the correct answer to complete each sentence.

EXAMPLE:

Mark _____ a headache last night.　　Ⓐ B C D
   (A) had　　　　　　　　　(C) has had
   (B) has　　　　　　　　　(D) was having

1. That novel was written _____ Amy Tan.　　A B C D
   (A) at　　　　　　　　　(C) from
   (B) by　　　　　　　　　(D) to

2. **A:** Do you cut your own hair?　　A B C D
   B: No. I _____.
   (A) cut it　　　　　　　(C) have it cut
   (B) have cut it　　　　　(D) haven't

3. This magazine _____ by many people.　　A B C D
   (A) are read　　　　　　(C) is reading
   (B) is read　　　　　　　(D) reads

4. _____ these books published in Europe?　　A B C D
   (A) Do　　　　　　　　　(C) Was
   (B) Have　　　　　　　　(D) Were

5. **A:** When _____ it built?　　A B C D
   B: In 1960.
   (A) does　　　　　　　　(C) is
   (B) has　　　　　　　　　(D) was

6. Cotton _____ in the southern part of　　A B C D
the country.
   (A) is produced　　　　　(C) produced
   (B) is producing　　　　　(D) produces

7. The report _____ soon.　　A B C D
   (A) publishes　　　　　　(C) will be published
   (B) is published　　　　　(D) will publish

8. **A:** When will the work be completed?　　　　　　　　　　**A　B　C　D**
   B: It _____ be done by June, but I'm not really sure.
   (A) has　　　　　　　　　　　(C) will
   (B) might　　　　　　　　　　(D) won't

9. How often _____ your car serviced since you bought it?　**A　B　C　D**
   (A) do you get　　　　　　　　(C) had you gotten
   (B) did you get　　　　　　　 (D) have you gotten

10. I think she usually _____ her own clothes.　　　　**A　B　C　D**
    (A) have made　　　　　　　　(C) is made
    (B) has them made　　　　　　(D) makes

PART TWO

DIRECTIONS: Each sentence has four underlined words or phrases. The four underlined parts of the sentence are marked A, B, C, and D. Circle the letter of the <u>one</u> underlined word or phrase that is NOT CORRECT.

EXAMPLE:

Rosa <u>rarely</u> <u>is using</u> public transportation, but <u>this morning</u> she　　**A Ⓑ C D**
　　　　A　　B　　　　　　　　　　　　　　　　C
<u>is taking</u> the bus.
　　D

11. That movie <u>was</u> <u>directed</u> <u>from</u> <u>someone</u> very well known.　　**A　B　C　D**
　　　　　　　A　　B　　　C　　D

12. Before a final decision <u>is reached</u>, the various possibilities　　**A　B　C　D**
　　　　　　　　　　　　A
　　<u>should</u> probably <u>discussed</u> <u>by</u> the whole team.
　　　　B　　　　　　C　　　D

13. I <u>used to</u> do my own taxes, <u>but</u> now I <u>have done them</u> <u>by</u> an　　**A　B　C　D**
　　　　A　　　　　　　　　B　　　　　C　　　　　D
　　accountant.

14. The house <u>painted</u> three years ago, but I'm not <u>going to</u> <u>have</u>　　**A　B　C　D**
　　　　　　　A　　　　　　　　　　　　　　　B　　C
　　<u>it done</u> again for a while.
　　　D

15. We <u>didn't</u> <u>know</u> about the problem so it <u>shouldn't</u> <u>be handled</u> in time.　**A　B　C　D**
　　　　A　　B　　　　　　　　　　C　　　D

16. A lot of crops <u>can't</u> be <u>grew</u> in the mountains because <u>it</u> <u>gets</u> too cold.　**A　B　C　D**
　　　　　　　A　　　　B　　　　　　　　　　C　D

17. That pottery <u>was</u> <u>found</u> <u>by</u> an archaeologist while she <u>was worked</u> in　**A　B　C　D**
　　　　　　　A　　B　　C　　　　　　　　　　　　D
　　this area.

18. When we <u>visit</u> Mexico, we<u>'re going to</u> <u>have</u> our pictures <u>took</u> on top   **A B C D**

              A   B   C   D

of an Aztec temple.

19. You <u>should</u> <u>be get</u> the locks <u>changed</u> after you <u>move</u> into a new   **A B C D**

            A   B   C   D

apartment.

20. <u>When</u> it <u>is launched</u>, the new space station <u>will</u> <u>be carried</u> an   **A B C D**

      A   B   C   D

international crew.

TEST: UNITS 21–24

DIRECTIONS: *Circle the letter of the correct answer to complete each sentence.*

EXAMPLE:

Mark _____ a headache last night.   (A) B C D
- (A) had
- (B) has
- (C) has had
- (D) was having

1. If you _____ any questions, ask.   A B C D
   - (A) are having
   - (B) had
   - (C) have
   - (D) will have

2. If you heat air, it _____.   A B C D
   - (A) is rising
   - (B) rise
   - (C) rises
   - (D) rose

3. _____ Fao-Shen visits Vancouver, she   A B C D
   stays with her aunt.
   - (A) Always
   - (B) During
   - (C) Ever
   - (D) Whenever

4. I'll call you if I _____ from Toby.   A B C D
   - (A) hear
   - (B) 'm hearing
   - (C) 'm going to hear
   - (D) will hear

5. What will you do if the letter _____   A B C D
   arrive by tomorrow?
   - (A) doesn't
   - (B) didn't
   - (C) won't
   - (D) wouldn't

6. _____ you have a license, you can't   A B C D
   drive in California.
   - (A) As
   - (B) If
   - (C) Unless
   - (D) When

7. If I _____ you, I'd call the doctor.   A B C D
   - (A) am
   - (B) was
   - (C) were
   - (D) would be

8. What would you do if you _____ the lottery?   **A   B   C   D**
   (A) 're winning   (C) won
   (B) win   (D) would win

9. I wish I _____ more free time.   **A   B   C   D**
   (A) had   (C) will have
   (B) have   (D) would have

10. **A:** If you knew the answer, would you tell me?   **A   B   C   D**
    B: Yes, I _____ .
    (A) did   (C) would
    (B) will   (D) would have

11. Where _____ you go if you wanted to rent a car?   **A   B   C   D**
    (A) can   (C) would
    (B) do   (D) would have

12. Now Don wishes he _____ studying English years ago.   **A   B   C   D**
    (A) had started   (C) starts
    (B) is starting   (D) started

13. If you _____ told us about the movie, we wouldn't have   **A   B   C   D**
    gone to see it.
    (A) didn't   (C) hadn't
    (B) wouldn't have   (D) haven't

14. The team _____ if the coach had let Tyler play.   **A   B   C   D**
    (A) can win   (C) could have won
    (B) can't win   (D) could win

PART TWO

DIRECTIONS: *Each sentence has four underlined words or phrases.*
The four underlined parts of the sentence are marked A, B, C, and D.
Circle the letter of the <u>one</u> underlined word or phrase that is NOT
CORRECT.

EXAMPLE:

Rosa <u>rarely</u> <u>is using</u> public transportation, but <u>this morning</u> she   **A Ⓑ C   D**
     A   B   C
<u>is taking</u> the bus.
   D

15. <u>If</u> Joan <u>had been</u> there yesterday, you <u>would have</u> <u>see</u> her.   **A   B   C   D**
     A   B   C   D

16. My mother <u>wishes</u> she <u>went</u> to medical school <u>when</u> she <u>was</u> younger.   **A   B   C   D**
                 A   B   C   D

17. I <u>would</u> <u>tell</u> her the truth <u>if</u> I <u>am</u> you.   **A   B   C   D**
       A   B   C   D

18. I <u>wish</u> our parents <u>could read</u> to us at bedtime <u>when</u> <u>we</u> were little. **A B C D**
      A   B   C   D

19. Our plans won't <u>work</u> <u>unless</u> we all don't <u>try</u> <u>harder</u>. **A B C D**
                 A   B   C   D

20. <u>If</u> you hadn't <u>driven</u> me to the station I <u>might not</u> <u>of</u> caught the train. **A B C D**
    A   B   C   D

TEST: UNITS 25–29

DIRECTIONS: *Circle the letter of the correct answer to complete each sentence.*

EXAMPLE:

Mark _____ a headache last night.   (Ⓐ) **B   C   D**
    (A) had   (C) has had
    (B) has   (D) was having

1. **A:** Is the restaurant around here?   **A   B   C   D**
   B: I'm not sure where _____.
   (A) is it   (C) it was
   (B) it is   (D) was it

2. "Do you know word processing?"   **A   B   C   D**
   Last week my employer asked me
   _____ I knew word processing.
   (A) did   (C) how
   (B) do   (D) if

3. Ann's friends all asked her why _____ **A   B   C   D**
   that job.
   (A) did she accept   (C) she had accepted
   (B) did you accept   (D) she accepts

4. **A:** What is that man's name?   **A   B   C   D**
   B: I'm not sure what _____.
   (A) his name   (C) 's his name
   (B) his name is   (D) was his name

5. We'd better find out _____ the bus **A   B   C   D**
   has left.
   (A) did   (C) has
   (B) does   (D) if

6. **A:** Should we turn left or right here?   **A   B   C   D**
   B: Hmm. I'm not certain which way _____.
   (A) do we turn   (C) to turn
   (B) should we turn   (D) turns

7. He _____, "The rent is due on the first of the month."　　**A　B　C　D**
   (A) asked
   (B) said
   (C) told
   (D) wanted to know

8. **Expert to reporter:** "Weather patterns change. We all agree　　**A　B　C　D**
   about that."
   Newspaper story: Experts say that weather
   patterns _____.
   (A) change
   (B) changed
   (C) were changing
   (D) had changed

9. **A:** I read your report.　　**A　B　C　D**
   B: Oh. What did you think of it?
   Al told Barbara that he had read _____ report.
   (A) her
   (B) his
   (C) my
   (D) your

10. Ten years ago, Tanya told John that she _____ to him again.　　**A　B　C　D**
    (A) has never spoken
    (B) never speaks
    (C) will never speak
    (D) would never speak

11. The police officer told us _____.　　**A　B　C　D**
    (A) stop
    (B) stopped
    (C) stopping
    (D) to stop

12. She asked us _____ so loud because the baby was sleeping.　　**A　B　C　D**
    (A) don't speak
    (B) not to speak
    (C) speak
    (D) to speak

PART TWO

DIRECTIONS: Each sentence has four underlined words or phrases. The four underlined parts of the sentence are marked A, B, C, and D. Circle the letter of the <u>one</u> underlined word or phrase that is NOT CORRECT.

EXAMPLE:

Rosa <u>rarely</u> <u>is using</u> public transportation, but <u>this morning</u> she　　**A　Ⓑ　C　D**
　　　 A　　　 B　　　　　　　　　　　　 C
<u>is taking</u> the bus.
　　 D

13. The teacher <u>said</u> the class <u>that</u> helium <u>is</u> lighter <u>than</u> oxygen.　　**A　B　C　D**
　　　　　　　 A　　　　　 B　　　　　 C　　　　 D

14. At 9:00 P.M. last Friday, my boss <u>called</u> me and <u>told</u> me I <u>have to</u> go　　**A　B　C　D**
　　　　　　　　　　　　　　　　 A　　　　　　 B　　　　 C
into the office <u>the next day</u>.
　　　　　　　 D

15. I'll never forget March 1971, <u>when</u> I <u>heard</u> on the radio <u>that</u> a   **A B C D**
                            A   B   C

     hurricane <u>is coming</u>.
               D

16. Gloria <u>called</u> me last week to <u>tell me</u> that she <u>needed</u> the   **A B C D**
             A   B   C

     information right <u>now</u>.
                 D

17. We <u>invited</u> <u>her</u> <u>visit</u> our class <u>last semester</u>.   **A B C D**
          A   B   C   D

18. Bob <u>asked</u> <u>me</u> <u>if or not</u> I <u>wanted</u> to go.   **A B C D**
         A   B   C   D

19. <u>Yesterday</u>, someone <u>asked</u> me <u>how</u> I pronounced my <u>name?</u>   **A B C D**
       A   B   C   D

20. <u>Could</u> you <u>tell</u> me <u>what time</u> <u>is it</u>?   **A B C D**
       A   B   C   D

ANSWER KEY FOR TESTS

Correct responses for Part Two questions appear in parentheses.

ANSWER KEY FOR TEST: UNITS 1–4

PART ONE
1. B	7. B
2. A	8. D
3. A	9. D
4. C	10. B
5. C	11. D
6. C	12. D

PART TWO
13. D (were sleeping)	17. D (saw)
14. C (named)	18. D (graduated)
15. C (changed)	19. B (hadn't)
16. B (got)	20. A (have)

ANSWER KEY FOR TEST: UNITS 5–6

PART ONE
1. B	6. C
2. B	7. A
3. B	8. D
4. A	9. C
5. D	10. B

PART TWO
11. B (be)
12. B (washes)
13. B (finish)
14. C ('ll call OR 's going to call OR 'll be calling)
15. A (will have been saving)
16. A (have)
17. D (working)
18. D (for)
19. C (paid)
20. D (carried)

ANSWER KEY FOR TEST: UNITS 7–8

PART ONE
1. A	8. C
2. C	9. B
3. A	10. A
4. B	11. B
5. C	12. B
6. A	13. A
7. B	14. A

PART TWO
15. D (it)	18. C (but)
16. D (she)	19. C (didn't)
17. D (did)	20. D (is Craig)

ANSWER KEY FOR TEST: UNITS 9–10

PART ONE
1. D	7. D
2. B	8. C
3. D	9. A
4. D	10. D
5. A	11. B
6. C	12. D

PART TWO
13. B (to help)
14. A (to change)
15. C (trying)
16. A (of)
17. B (finding)
18. D (to return)
19. D (of losing OR to lose)
20. D (to buy)

ANSWER KEY FOR TEST:
UNITS 11–12

PART ONE

1. A
2. A
3. D
4. A
5. A
6. A
7. A
8. D
9. C
10. D
11. B

PART TWO

12. A (it over)
13. D (up)
14. D (off the bus)
15. D (back OR over)
16. D (up in a dictionary)
17. B (get on the bus)
18. D (off)
19. A (up)
20. B (cheer her up)

ANSWER KEY FOR TEST:
UNITS 13–14

PART ONE

1. B
2. B
3. D
4. D
5. A
6. D
7. B
8. B
9. D
10. C
11. D
12. D

PART TWO

13. B *(delete)*
14. B (whose)
15. B *(delete* OR that OR which)
16. D *(delete)*
17. C (discuss)
18. B (which)
19. A (who)
20. B (work)

ANSWER KEY FOR TEST:
UNITS 15–17

PART ONE

1. B
2. C
3. C
4. A
5. D
6. D
7. B
8. D
9. C
10. C
11. D
12. D
13. B
14. A

PART TWO

15. C (have)
16. B (have)
17. B (have)
18. D (must not have OR couldn't have)
19. D (rented)
20. B (close)

ANSWER KEY FOR TEST:
UNITS 18–20

PART ONE

1. B
2. C
3. B
4. D
5. D
6. A
7. C
8. B
9. D
10. D

PART TWO

11. C (by)
12. C (be discussed)
13. C (have them done)
14. A (was painted)
15. C (couldn't)
16. B (grown)
17. D (was working OR worked)
18. D (taken)
19. B (get)
20. D (carry)

ANSWER KEY FOR TEST:
UNITS 21–24

PART ONE

1. C
2. C
3. D
4. A
5. A
6. C
7. C
8. C
9. A
10. C
11. C
12. A
13. C
14. C

PART TWO

15. D (seen)
16. B (had gone)
17. D (were)
18. B (could have read)
19. B (if)
20. D (have)

ANSWER KEY FOR TEST:
UNITS 25–29

PART ONE

1. B
2. D
3. C
4. B
5. D
6. C
7. B
8. A
9. A
10. D
11. D
12. B

PART TWO

13. A (told OR said to)
14. C (had to)
15. D (was coming)
16. D (then)
17. C (to visit)
18. C (whether or not OR if)
19. D (name.)
20. D (it is)